The White Anglo-Saxon Protestant Bachelor's Survival Guide and Cookbook

The White Anglo-Saxon Protestant Bachelor's Survival Guide and Cookbook

Jeff Clothier
With Illustrations by
David Phipps

iUniverse, Inc.
New York Lincoln Shanghai

The White Anglo-Saxon Protestant Bachelor's Survival Guide and Cookbook

iUniverse, Inc.

For information address:
iUniverse, Inc.
2021 Pine Lake Road, Suite 100
Lincoln, NE 68512
www.iuniverse.com

ISBN: 0-595-32447-9 (pbk)
ISBN: 0-595-66583-7 (cloth)

Printed in the United States of America

For Jill.

Finally, somebody to laugh with.

Contents

Foreword

By Pat Blank, Senior News Producer
90.9 FM KUNI Radio, Cedar Falls, Iowa

I've known Jeff Clothier since 1995, when, in an act of pure shameless self-promotion, he emailed the radio station suggesting we add him to our list of weekend commentators. Blissfully ignorant or boldly arrogant, he persisted, even after my obligatory reply informing him that we weren't in the market for anyone. We already had your standard cast of characters covering the political spectrum, arts and literature, and other random musings I edited and aired both because I enjoyed working with these folks, and because the government said we had to. But what we needed, according to Jeff, was comic relief. He sent a script and offered to add his voice to it "for our consideration."

As fate would have it, one of the usual suspects moved away, so we thought we'd give this brash young kid a chance. Much to our delight, our listeners welcomed his pithy mixture of satire and warmth with open arms, ears, and hearts. Eventually, so did we.

In the course of eight years, transcripts of Jeff's material were requested and sent, and we even forwarded tapes of his work to a loyal fan in California. He won two awards from the Iowa Associated Press, which made us look awfully good here at the station, let me tell you.

This book is sprinkled throughout with the same quirky wit I looked forward to each time Jeff and I met at the "Big T Maidrite" in Toledo, Iowa to chew on burnt English muffin toast, gossip, then retreat to the Big Red Rolling Recording Studio (my trusty Chevy pickup) to lay down some prime Clothier commentary. Treat yourself to a copy.

Then treat your friends by inviting Jeff to speak to your favorite service organization or civic group. He's a veteran Toastmaster, so what he delivers will be anything but burnt toast!

CROCK
POT

CRACK
POT

Purpose and Credentials

Despite the title, I promise you this book is neither racist nor sexist—neither is the author, particularly. But ever since Mrs. Claussen's senior English class I've been told over and over again to write what I know. Since I just happen to *be* a white, Anglo-Saxon Protestant bachelor (hereafter to be known as a "WASPB"), everything you read will necessarily come from that unique and profound point of view.

First, let me state that we WASPBs are a much-maligned, oft-ignored minority. Yes, I said minority.

Think about it. Last statistics I read put women at fifty-two percent of the population. Fifty-two percent! Men, therefore, bring up the rear with a measly forty-eight percent. Now to my mind, that constitutes a minority, albeit a pretty big one.

Now, subtract from that forty-eight percent those who are consistently non-Caucasian, non-Teutonic, non-Calvinist and married, and what you've got left over is a pretty geeky bunch of guys who don't dance well, have a hard time getting a date, and who honestly believe their Oedipus complex constitutes emotional well being. I think a book of this type is desperately needed. I certainly wish I'd had it to refer to after I got out of college. I would have avoided many a lethal meal and countless crippled pairs of socks.

You see, I got married in 1989 and realized immediately that I needed to learn how to cook. After the divorce, I moved to another city. For an Emancipation Day present, my saintly grandmother (I said "saintly," not "sainted." My grandmother is still very much alive, thank you, although she threatens to keel over daily unless I manage to produce some great-grandchildren somehow. Cloning, maybe?) bought me a "Crock-Pot®" (Marca Registrada, the Rival Corporation).

Doubly armed with an efficiency-sized microwave, I have since become an expert in slow and fast cooking. Normal speed I still have trouble with, and I have absolutely no idea what to do with my oven, but I can make microwaved fryer parts taste like a Texas barbecue. (This is a blatant plug for my first recipe: "Texas Mesquite Nuclear Chicken," which ought to be along in a page or two.) Or, I can slip it into the slow cooker all day on low, and come home to eminently palatable chicken soup.

A strange thing happened to me the other day. Out of the blue, a thirteen-year-old boy skateboarded up to me and requested an interview. When I asked him why, he said, "My folks are cheesed off at me 'cause I say 'That's women's work' whenever they tell me to do something around the house, so they said I had to go out and talk to a real man."

"Well, Jimmy," I said, "you've come to the right place. I live alone. If I don't cook, I don't eat. If I don't do laundry, my socks stink. If I don't vacuum, at least semiannually, erosion patterns begin to form in my carpet."

"What's your point?" Jimmy said snottily.

Consequently, this book is aimed at adults.

Nevertheless, the points I make are valid. More and more of us these days are single-person families, our own dependants, lone strangers by choice or chance. If we can't always enjoy the situation, we can at least learn to cope with it.

I'm a forty-something Lutheran white guy from Iowa. I've been a teacher, a musician, a writer, a communications professional with a god-awfully huge biotech company, a website designer, a public radio commentator, a small business owner and sometime housepainter. I've practiced serial monogamy for going on twenty years now. In between marriages and relationships—both serious and spurious—I've relied on my skills as a single male homemaker and honed them to a fine point. I can cook things that don't come out of a can, keep my clothes and surroundings relatively neat and clean, and cope comfortably with waking up to no company but my own for extended periods of time. Despite any number of self-imposed setbacks, I've gotten by okay and generally come up smiling—occasionally, even grinning.

But it hasn't been easy.

Trouble is there's no manual for this sort of thing, at least not one a guy can be caught reading at the barbershop or while waiting for his tires to be rotated. I've mostly had to feel my way, which isn't as much fun as it sounds. I've had glorious triumphs and spectacular failures. Most guys do. The only difference is I've written them down. As a writer and former teacher, I feel a responsibility to pass on what little I've learned to the next generation of sweatshirt-wearing, used–car-driving, apartment-trashing, career-seeking malcontents and low self-esteem sufferers.

But back to racism.

I mentioned earlier that as a practicing WASPB, I can't write from, say, the point of view of a Senegalese transgendered Mormon. No way could I pull it off and be convincing. But in choosing my audience, I thought about the black guys I knew in college. To a man, these fellows appeared poised and confident, relaxed and capable in any social situation. Lord knows they had all the women.

I also had quite a few friends from Southeast Asia, the majority of whom were capable of living for weeks at a time on a cabbage and a single change of clothes. Besides, they studied so doggone much I don't think they ever stopped to notice whether or not they were hungry. Still, they did much of their own cooking, and wisely gave the cafeteria a wide berth.

We white guys, frankly, have no cultural direction. Our women are no help. We're supposed to be sensitive, yet virile, politically correct, yet commanding and aggressive. Our mothers tell us one thing, our girlfriends another, and never the twain shall meet, God willing. The girls we encounter want to date James Dean but marry John Ritter, so we spend most of our Caucasian youth trying to establish a persona that nine times out of ten comes out like "Rebel Without A Penis."

So I offer this slim volume of accumulated wisdom to all single white males and to the women trying gallantly to love them. It's also a handy manual for friends, family, coworkers, and anyone else trying to get a handle on just what the heck's wrong with us.

In short, this book's for everybody.

It's the story of one Midwestern white guy's slow, fitful climb toward maturity and independence with all the screw-ups included. If you pay attention, you may just get a laugh or six as you learn to avoid the many, many pitfalls I dug for myself, then stumbled into.

We'll cover things like hunting for a job, an apartment, the money missing from your paycheck every month, and your next relationship. You'll learn how to keep your room clean safely and why. You'll learn some easy and mostly edible recipes, and here and there I'll even throw in some free advice. Wow, talk about value for the money!

So now you know pretty much what this book's about, who it's for, what my credentials are for writing it, and that I'm not a racist. We're ready for our first recipe.

TEXAS MESQUITE NUCLEAR CHICKEN

Ingredients:

• 1 small, medium, or large chicken, or various parts thereof

• 1 onion, any kind or color

• 1 green bell pepper, any kind or color

• 1 bottle, any brand, mesquite flavor barbecue sauce

• Beer. Lots of beer. Any kind or color.

Directions:

Chop everything up but the beer; dump in microwave on high for 25 mins. Serves 1 or more.

That's it.

"That's it?" you say incredulously?

Of course! The first rule of WASPB-hood is K.I.S.S.—"Keep It Simple, Stupid!" You start throwing in a lot of unnecessary complications, and you end up wasting a lot of time, a lot of food, and a lot of money eating drive-thru Zippyburgers and kosher pizza.

You were expecting, maybe, Emeril Lagasse?

Boyz II Mensch

From what you've read so far, you've probably gotten the impression that I didn't learn how to take care of myself until after my erstwhile marriage. This is a blatant lie.

My mother will tell you—whether you want her to it or not—that my sister and I were both pretty much self-sufficient by age eight, and that's true. We helped cook, did dishes—even an occasional load of laundry. As a matter of fact, the only thing I ever needed a girl for in the first place was...

But I digress.

My parents both worked outside the home—an arrangement we all found both convenient and emotionally satisfying despite right-wing propaganda to the contrary. So, naturally, my sibling and I were trained early and often.

FREE ADVICE No.1: WASPBs, if you are contemplating marriage, co-habitation, or even heavy petting, do not, I repeat, DO NOT tell your intended any of the things you learn from this book.

See, women want you to *need* them to take care of you, even if they have no earthly intention of actually doing so. Get it? Neither did I. Need I say more?

When I got to college, I neglected to call home for the first several weeks. My poor folks had no idea whether I was spending my time in the library or the local pub. When they finally got hold of me, I explained that since the first of September, I had been down in the laundry room patiently pointing out to each and every guy on my corridor that they could not put their white, cutaway, low-rise briefs in with their red and gold Iowa State warm-up suits. I don't know if you've ever spotted a herd of jock roaming the halls in pink underwear, but if you had, you'd certainly remember.

The folks forgave me, and promised to send money for more Clorox.

I soon found time to study because, by the end of the first quarter, most of the fellows had either learned to do for themselves, become resigned to permanent grubbiness, or found a girlfriend—preferably one working on her Mrs. degree.

FREE ADVICE No. 2: The worst enemy one WASPB can have is another WASPB.

We are such needy, greedy creatures that the competition for the necessities of life—food, clothing, shelter, sex, or the money to purchase same—can get pretty fierce. What with the Alpha males preying on the Beta males, and the Gammas being passive-aggressive all over the place, honestly, it's a jungle out there.

My first roommate was a bigot from Green Bay. He and his hairy-knuckled friends referred to me affectionately as "Hey, Music Faggot!"

and threatened to beat the crap out of me at regular intervals. This was *after* I had shown them how to do their laundry.

How this crew ever got into a Lutheran, liberal arts school I'll never know. They were anything but liberal, had nothing but contempt for the arts, and their Christianity was highly questionable. They developed a grudging respect for me, however, after I bagged one of the hottest babes on campus. See, being a WASPB can have an upside!

I often wonder what small-town insurance office, used-car dealership or flyblown townie bar those guys inhabit now. On the other hand, who cares? They probably all voted for Bush if they voted at all, and history will forget them, too.

The roommate situation got consistently better after that. At the beginning of my sophomore year, I got a different Wisconsinite, who taught me how to drink beer, and a physical therapy major from Colorado who joined us in drunkenly serenading the Evangelicals next door. At three o'clock each weekday afternoon, it was our pleasant custom to nosh on chocolate-chip cookies and beer while watching reruns of "I Dream of Jeannie." The next year I hooked up with a twerp of a premed who, for some reason, was a real babe magnet and graciously let me benefit from the fallout. Life was truly grand.

Now let's get one thing straight: College life is *not* bachelorhood. Your parents may not actually be there, but their surrogates are; and they may not see your every transgression, but they do grade them. Call it a dress rehearsal for true WASPBhood and you'll be inching closer to the truth.

But all good things must come to an end, and so did my carefree college days. The time came when I at last had to face the grim realities. I then made one of the most profound decisions of my life, and one that has colored my existence ever since: I moved back home.

It is increasingly common for adult children of employed parents to return to the backwater from which they were spawned. They may find themselves occupationally challenged (read that "unemployed"), as I was, or run into unforeseen personal difficulties that cause them to run home to their mommies. In my case, the problem was simply poor timing.

I had earned a teaching certificate in instrumental music (band), but, unlike my fellow music majors, I elected to do my student teaching during the marching band season in the fall following my graduation. This let me out at Christmas, smack in the middle of the school year and a lousy time to look for a teaching job. As a result, my first paid position as a college graduate was counter man in a donut shop.

One of my steady customers was a state Supreme Court justice. You'd be amazed how much free time the man had on his hands. He hung out every day with the farmers and retirees at five a.m. and again at three in the afternoon, and tried his best to beat me out of free coffee refills, citing the Iowa Constitution whenever he ran out of arguments. When he'd finally leave, he would invariably squint at me in my dingy white apron and jaunty paper hat and ask me frankly if this was the best I could do with my life.

Anyway, there I was, back in the nest in the old hometown, with everyone I ever knew stopping by to find out what donuts fried by a four-and-a half-year liberal arts graduate tasted like. Depressed? I should hope to shout.

It's no accident that the word "food" rhymes with "mood." Recipes appropriate to happy times tend to have chipper, sunny titles. Comfort food often does not. Here's a little number I used to inflict on my folks as often as I could get away with it, especially when I was in a particularly foul temper.

JEFF'S GRAY CROCK-POT SLUDGE

Ingredients:

- 1 can green beans, regular or French cut (for the adventurous)

- 1 can cream of mushroom soup

- 1 small pkg. Tater Tots

- 1 lb. lean ground beef, or use hamburger instead

- Onions, garlic, salt, pepper, whatever...

Directions:

- Brown the hamburger. (That is, cook it until it falls apart and turns gray. You'll be forever waiting for it to actually turn brown. You can do this in a skillet on the stove, although I wouldn't recommend it. Better to stick it in the microwave on medium high for a few minutes, and then drain the grease. Oh, yes, there *will* be grease.)

- Prepare Tater Tots as per pkg. directions, assuming you haven't already thrown away the pkg.

- Place meat, beans, soup and seasonings in crock-pot and arrange Tots on top.

- Turn crock-pot on low, leave the house for several hours and pray.

I love this one. It uses both my favorite appliances and, more often than not, tastes pretty good, especially when the chips are down and one craves a culinary hug.

My ex-wife, whom we will call "Doris," although her real name is Rosalind, had one good recipe in her repertoire. The girl made a mean lasagna. I still get nostalgic for Doris' lasagna from time to time. On the other hand, how often can you eat lasagna?

Unfortunately, I was not awarded custody of the lasagna recipe in the settlement, so I'm afraid I can't share it with you. Here's hoping the sludge pans out for you—no pun intended.

A WASPB Is Born

Between graduation and my not-so-triumphant homecoming, I was initiated into the rites of the single man during my student teaching assignment. The fall after my commencement, I moved nine miles down the road from my alma mater to a small town that was the center of a rural consolidated school district. I was pretty confident of my teaching skills, but it was surviving on my own that would prove the true education.

I arrived with all my belongings flung into the hatchback of one of those awful, mid-eighties, wide-bodied domestic cars that looked like the last-place finisher in a soapbox derby and sucked gasoline like a sperm whale sucks shrimp. The first thing I had to do was go to the local police station and give a statement. Seems this girl I'd dated the semester before (and who just happened to live in this particular hamlet) had gotten herself into a jam and couldn't think of anybody else to call.

When the constables were through with me, I heaved a sigh of relief and prepared to move into My First Apartment.

My landlords-to-be were a semiretired couple by the name of Morgan. Mrs. M. ran a beauty shop in her basement, catering mainly to the blue-rinse crowd, while her husband took his retirement much more seriously.

I had spoken to them once over the phone a couple weeks after the local Lutheran minister recommended them to me—any port in a storm. I rented their upstairs apartment sight-unseen.

No one was home to meet me when I arrived, but a futile-looking skeleton key had been left under the mat in typical, Midwest fashion. I let myself in and climbed a polished oak staircase adorned with a beautiful banister worn to a mellow glow by generations of hands and youthful backsides. At the top and down a short hallway were three doors: one to the right, one to the left, and one straight ahead. I looked around for Monty Hall.

The hallway was directly underneath the eaves so that the ceiling slanted down and to the left at an alarming angle. Vintage floral wallpaper adorned the walls.

I was a bit leery, realizing that I would have to go right past the Morgan's living room to get upstairs. Once I figured out they were both deaf as a post, I felt better about it. I later learned that deafness is often a voluntary thing among the elderly—a convenience they can turn on and off at will.

I grasped the center doorknob in breathless anticipation.

Lucky for me it was breathless, for as soon as I opened the door, the odor of ammonia slapped me in the face like a sexually harassed receptionist and made me gag. When I could finally open my eyes, I saw an old-fashioned kitchen with a quaint, three-burner gas range, ugly Formica countertops, and a small dinette table at the far end with one leg missing.

Pots, pans, utensils, scraps of yellowed newspaper, rags, cleaning supplies, cans of bug killer, burned out light bulbs, and a number of empty one-gallon ice cream buckets lay strewn about the counters and all over the floor. What a mess! It looked like the previous tenants had bugged out an hour ago owing several months back rent.

My landlady appeared in the doorway. For a beauty operator, she had a pretty deranged "do." Sort of a cross between a fifties bouffant and a medieval monk's tonsure.

"Sorry about the mess," she said. "I was cleaning out the cupboards and sort of got away from it."

She wiped her cellophane glove-clad hand off on her aquamarine, 100 percent polyester slacks and shook one of mine with it.

"I'm Mrs. Morgan," she said.

She took me through the place; a tour that lasted approximately twenty seconds. The bedroom/living room combination was really quite lovely—mostly antique furniture and ornaments. The mattress and spring of the enormous old bed were well over hip-high, with a hand-quilted comforter and bolster. The headboard was an impressive mass of carved mahogany. A matching dresser with beveled mirror stood by. The couch and non-coordinated chairs of the living room were early garage sale, but after the disaster in the kitchen, it all looked like paradise.

Mrs. Morgan cleared her throat and said she had a "permanent cooking down cellar." (A permanent *what*, I wondered.) She reminded me that the rent was due on the twentieth of the month, and left me to unpack. I dumped my stuff on the bed. Things could've been worse.

As I grew more familiar with my surroundings—and they with me—I realized what I'd lucked into. The bay window in the living room jutted out between the limbs of a spreading chestnut tree. I spent quite a lot of time sitting there watching it turn all Fourth-of-July as the fall fell.

The Morgans had a garden out back, and every few days I'd find a grocery sack full of fresh sweet corn, squash, or tomatoes on the stairway, and at least once a day, one or the other of these kindly spirits stopped to ask if I needed anything. My landfolks were fond of me.

> Free Advice No. 3: While it is important to get along with on-premises landlords, one can certainly overdo it.

The Morgans soon took to calling my parents whenever I would bring "friends" over or deviate in any way from what they considered a proper routine for a young, unmarried schoolmaster. This was great for my folks, who now had their very own Distant Early Warning System in place.

There were other drawbacks to my living arrangements as well. The place had an ancient gas boiler in the basement and steam heat, over which I had no control. In the winter, I alternately froze and roasted, often going through several cycles a night. The gas had to be coaxed to the top floor of the house, and it would often take the better part of an hour just to boil water on the stove or brew coffee.

Plus, the sanitary facilities were outside the apartment proper in a small, closet-like space under the eaves in the hallway. The sharply slanted ceiling made it necessary to cock my head to the right when performing my bodily function—a habit that sneaks up on me from time to time, even now.

It also meant that the whole house could hear when I was "awake in the night." Amazing how two elderly people who can't hear the phone ring across the room can zero in on someone peeing one floor up at three o'clock in the morning. One or the other of them would invariably holler up the stairs to see if I was all right. I wondered if past generations of renters had enjoyed this nightly ritual, or if the Morgans had initiated it just for me.

Probably the biggest inconvenience was when I allowed myself to be guilt-tripped into singing at the Morgan's church. It would be a nice gesture, I rationalized to myself, and since the church was right next door, I figured it wouldn't put me out too much.

Then I found out that the reverend had arranged to have his Sunday services broadcast over local radio. Seems he fancied himself a young Robert Schuller, only his choir was ghastly, so he frequently shanghaied innocent young music majors like myself into saving his pastoral butt.

I became a weekly feature, and somewhat of a local celeb, but it also killed quite a few weeknights in futile rehearsals with the choir and Mrs. Gatsby, the world-famous ten-thumbed pianist. Thus began and ended my spotty career as a gospel singer.

One day, along with the usual care package on the steps, I found two frozen lamb chops wrapped in butcher paper. Mrs. Morgan was saying "thank you" for driving one of her little old clients home from her wash and set when her ne'er-do-well son failed to pick her up.

My microwave oven, you must understand, was still a future blessing, so here's what I did with the chops:

LAMB CHOPS A L'ORANGE

Ingredients:

• Two lamb chops

• 1 can mandarin oranges in juice

• Salt, oregano, paprika—anything to take the curse off the oranges

Directions:

• Place lamb chops in small roaster.

• Cover with oranges and about half the juice.

• Bake in antique gas oven with stingy fuel supply for about two hours.

• Season to taste. Believe me, you'll need to.

Obviously, this wasn't one of my more successful concoctions. I ended up scraping all the orange goop off and salting the hell out of the chops, but it was all I had in the house. I experimented quite a lot in this vein: Sardines au Gratin, Corn Flakes in Pesto Sauce—that sort of thing. Even Chef Boyardee had to start somewhere, right?

At that point I was more like Chef Boy-Ar-Don't.

Squatter's Rites

Never having lived alone before, I found I had to establish some sort of routine. I'm not saying the one I stumbled onto was particularly efficient, but it sort of worked. I had to be at school at 7:30, and the car I was driving strenuously objected to being awakened early, particularly on frosty autumn mornings. Plus, the natural gas situation made it necessary to plan coffee-making on a calendar.

I typically arose between 5:30 and 6:00 and immediately turned on the stove, having put fresh coffee and water into the old granite-steel coffeepot the night before. I would stumble toward what I came to refer to as the "toilet closet," being unaware at the time of the common British term "water closet," effectively waking up the entire house. Did I mention that the plumbing sang like Mahalia Jackson, Michael Jackson, and the Mormon Tabernacle Choir with every flush?

Then I'd jump into the shower, which was in a separate, pantry-like alcove off the kitchen. The hot water typically lasted about six minutes and dribbled disconsolately down on me from the incorrectly installed showerhead. The aluminum enclosure was just barely wide enough to stand in, and I performed my ablutions moving rhythmically from side to side trying to catch the largest, warmest drops.

Emerging from the stall like Houdini out of a steamer trunk, I'd check in the mirror for places I'd failed to rinse. Nine times out of ten, I'd end up leaving the house with little gobs of shampoo clinging to the back of my neck.

By this time, the coffee was just beginning to think about perking. After I'd shaved and dressed, it would have begun to bubble morosely. Sort of "Flub-up...*sigh*. Flub-up...*sigh*." I'd pour my cornflakes and a Flintstones jelly glass full of juice, sit at the little three-legged table staring at the coffeepot, and make encouraging noises whenever it gave out with a particularly enthusiastic perk. On a good day, I'd get half a grainy, tepid cup down before I had to leave.

I remember coming home one particularly cruddy day, during which my cooperating teacher had asked me: "Do you know how to restring French horn valves?" I lied and said I did. "Good," he said, and pointed me toward a shelf of no less than twenty instruments of the Baroque era.

"Restring those, willya?" he said, crossing his feet upon his desk and pouring himself a hearty cupful from the filth-encrusted Bunn-O-Matic nearby. I finished around nightfall, thanks to some encouragement and a spool of fishing line proffered by a friendly janitor.

As I stepped into my kitchen that night, something went "splash." It was the sound of my foot being engulfed in a puddle the size and relative pure-water content of Lake Erie.

I turned on the light and discovered several odd things. One, the door of the tiny freezer on top of the fridge was open. Two, the moisture sluicing down the front of the appliance and forming the pond in the middle of the kitchen floor was nearly black. And, three, something smelled like the day after a stock car race.

The Morgans, bless them, promptly replaced the refrigerator/ freezer. The problem had something to do with the automatic defrost shorting out and Freon tubes bursting—your basic Frigidaire Armageddon. But there wasn't much they could do about the eighty dollars worth of hamburger, chicken wings and frozen waffles that were supposed to have kept body and soul together until Christmas.

Oh, I got by quite well on care packages from home, but as the Morgans and I were cleaning up the mess, I noticed my landlady sort of sniffing the air and mentally white-gloving everything. After living there for more than a month, I finally noticed—the place was dirty! This was an epiphany similar to the time in junior high school when I accepted Jesus as my personal Savior, and was baptized in the Blood and with Fire by a young woman who would later be institutionalized, and whose husband ran off with the shortstop on the local girl's softball team.

Mrs. Morgan had once shown me where there was a vacuum cleaner I could use, but I couldn't remember, so I asked her again. She gave me a look I hadn't seen since I took piano lessons from my Aunt Viola, and referred me to the hall closet. She also pointed out that there were cleaning supplies under my kitchen sink, "In case you haven't run across them yet."

FREE ADVICE No. 4: If you're not sure what to do with household chemicals, at least be aware of what not to do, *i.e.* DO NOT MIX THEM.

I decided to start on the kitchen and bathroom floors—the topsoil on each being thick enough by now to support an herb garden, with the kitchen, of course, now being quite well irrigated. My hair at that time was about shoulder length, and loose follicles were everywhere, making the bathroom floor look like a Turkish rug that had come unraveled.

I grabbed an empty ice cream bucket and decided this job called for both ammonia *and* Clorox.

When I came to, I noticed that a powdery white sediment had settled in the bottom of the bucket. I couldn't remember mopping the floor, so I guessed that the bucket had been dirty to begin with. I flushed the mixture down the stool.

I later learned that that sediment is one of the simpler recipes for homemade high explosive, and a staple in cheap spy novels and mercenary magazines. I even read a short story once where a guy killed his father by pouring bleach into the toilet tank, ammonia into the bowl, and waiting for Papa to flush. I resolved to proceed more cautiously, and stick to ammonia cleaner alone. My floors soon began to shine, and the fetid zoo aroma slowly retreated.

Dusting puzzled me. I remembered as a child seeing my mom spraying stuff on a rag and wiping down everything in the house that was made of wood, but the theory escaped me. Where does the dust actually go? If it just gets knocked off onto the floor, what's the point? Besides, the only aerosols I had in the place were underarm deodorant and a can of ant and roach killer. Neither seemed appropriate.

It took me most of a Saturday afternoon to clean an apartment the size of the average cockapoo's doghouse. The only thing I hadn't done was vacuum under the furniture. I figured that could wait. After all, the place looked clean, and mostly smelled that way, too. About halfway through the semester, I broke a leg off one of the living room chairs. When I upended it to see if it could be fixed, I found that the last few tenants had apparently taken the same attitude. I could have plowed and planted underneath that chair. And all this time I thought I'd had a cold.

I had a small party for my buddies and their significant others to celebrate my successful cleaning frenzy. I thought the customary twelve-pack a bit mundane—after all, we weren't in the dorms anymore. Unfortunately, I wasn't much of a bartender. I'd heard of mulled wine, figured it had to be similar to malted milk, and thought it sounded good for a crisp October evening:

JEFF'S MULLED-OVER WINE

Ingredients:

- 1 gal. jug red, rosé, or off-white wine

- 1 each: fresh orange, lemon, lime

- 1 container whole cloves

- 1 container stick cinnamon

- Sugar

Directions:

- Pour wine into large saucepan.

- Slice fruit into pan.

- Dump in cloves, cinnamon sticks.

- Bring to a slow, steamy boil.

- Turn heat down and simmer slowly for at least an hour.

- Strain, add sugar to taste; serve in punch glass or Dixie cup with cinnamon stick.

    Ah, civilization!

Family and Other Forces of Nature

As I mentioned before, we WASPBs tend to spend an inordinate amount of time with our relatives. This is another great reason to learn the domestic arts. You'll generally find your stays as a houseguest more pleasant and that awful, back-to-the-womb feeling somewhat mitigated if you can at least *appear* to pull your own weight.

And, as I said, at the end of my student teaching stint, jobs in my field were impossible to come by, so I was forced to go back to the one place in the world where they had no choice but to take me in. Home, sweet home.

Understand that most people on Earth have homes and families much more unpleasant than mine. In fact, most of the time the Clothier household had rather a *Father Knows Best* aura to it, with my mother playing Robert Young.

My dad was a hundred-mile commuter. Most nights of the week it was just my mom and me—a situation that would cause many a therapist to immediately raise his fee. I now look back on that period fondly, but at the time, having to crawl back home knocked my youthful male ego lower than it had been since "Locker Room Show-and-Tell" in junior high school.

Since my job at Daryl's Doughnuts didn't pay enough to let me pay rent, I paid in kind, taking on a big chunk of the cooking, cleaning, laundry and yardwork.

This was fine by my mother, whose job took her out on the road every day. By the time she got home, she was usually too exhausted and grumpy to lift a finger.

I found that one great way to ingratiate myself to the folks was to get up early and cook breakfast. I didn't do this very often—usually only on weekends, especially if my younger sister was home from her steady job to visit. (You can imagine what a kick in the crotch that was.)

If you try this, be sure to make a big, messy deal out of it. You'll find your efforts appreciated much more, and you'll probably never be asked to do it again.

In planning these morning meals, I hearkened back to some of the classic pancake feeds of my childhood. The family pancake breakfast is no less arcane a ritual than a Catholic high mass. There are certain requirements: The entire immediate family must be present, there must be plenty of unscheduled time afterward to clean up the mess, and the last such event must have occurred so far back in the mists of time that nobody remembers what a horror it was.

Mom would check her ingredients to see if we had enough flour, eggs, milk, butter, baking powder, pots, pans, power tools, Band-aids and Bactine to even *begin* a project of this magnitude.

"Wait a minute. What's the Bisquick doing in the freezer?"

"Shut up and break the eggs."

My mother owned the largest mixing bowl in the known universe. I say this because modern shelf and cupboard technology had so far to go to cope with the sheer size of this bowl, that I concluded it had to be of alien origin.

Mom never measured. By dead reckoning alone she'd slop just the right amount of everything into the big yellow bowl, sloshing it around with a wooden spoon like a cartoon witch.

She checked carefully for color and consistency. The proper color for good pancake batter, according to my mother, was the same as the off-white wallpaper in the master bedroom of my great-grandmother's house in Manning, Iowa—*circa* 1954. Pre-'54, the wallpaper had not yet mellowed to the luscious cream hue it now sports.

While this went on, Dad would get out the Dupont Silverstone Non-Stick Mega-Griddle and coat it with a delicate film of oil. He'd turn on the stove, inevitably the wrong burner, and half an hour later, move the pan over to the now cherry-red element and allow the oil to pop and fume for several minutes. To test for the correct temperature, he would then sprinkle cold water on the hot oil, spattering everyone, and causing third-degree burns.

Now for the big question: Who's going to cook? The perennial pancake tragedy is that one must fry so that others may eat. Usually, Mom would put the back of her hand to her forehead and vow to martyr herself once again for the sake of her hungry offspring. She'd pour the thickened batter into perfect circles with a coffee cup, which later would have to be chiseled from its armor of dried-on batter.

The first cakes typically came out thin, wan and crispy from being deep-fried in too much oil. The second were much better, but the third generation cakes were always closest to perfection.

Ah, those quintessential cakes of the third panful, oozing with butter and syrup, were the ones mouths had been watering over for hours. Golden brown on the outside, light and fluffy on the inside, these, the very Platonean ideal of pancakes slid down the gullet like a Scotch mist and made themselves at home.

And Mom never got any.

As soon as Dad had stuffed himself, he would graciously offer to trade places with his now-famished spouse. This was the moment we all dreaded—Dad's famous Rorschach pancakes. Hideous black discs that lay there on the plate defying butter to melt on them or syrup to cling.

To make them seem harmless, less cruel and forbidding, he would form them into cheerful, friendly shapes like Mickey Mouse or Donald Duck. Then he would bring his charred characters out on a plate and lay them in front of Mother like burnt offerings.

"See, Honey? It's Tweety Bird!"

"Thanks," Mom would say. "But I prefer to interpret them myself."

Sure, pancakes are a mess and a misery, but they're also quick and easy so there's no need to quote you a recipe—I think.

FREE ADVICE No. 5: If you're so inclined, pick up a few of those "shake and pour" batter mixes, disappear into the kitchen, and make lots of pan-clattering noises for about half an hour. Your family will love you for it.

Or, instead of flapjacks, try this omelet I adapted from the late TV chef, Julia Child. Julia cooked her omelets slowly over very low heat, declaring that before you add ingredients and flip them shut they must set up to a "lovely custard consistency."

I've gone Julia one better. My omelets generally *end up* in a lovely custard consistency. Hopefully you'll do much better.

JEFF & JULIA'S COLLABORATIVE OMELETTE

Ingredients:

- 1 doz. eggs (preferably hen's eggs)

- All the onions, peppers, garlic, salt, pepper left over from the previous recipes

- Grated cheese (Velveeta's for amateurs)

- Fresh mushrooms (from the store, not from the old tree stump out back)

Directions:

- Preheat lightly buttered frying pan on medium high.

- Crack eggs one at a time into a coffee cup. (Mom always made me do this. I have no idea why.)

- (Why am I always parenthesizing things in these recipes?)

- Pour eggs into mixing bowl and beat to a froth with a wire whisk, adding a little milk or water to "custardize" them.

- Pour eggs into pan and let set up for a few minutes.

- Make a thin bed of cheese, then add chopped up veggies.

- Using two spatulas, fold the whole thing up into the shape of a taco, and sprinkle more cheese on top.

Voila!

I was always a little worried about Julia. In her latter years on PBS, she acquired a partner named Jacques to do much of the manual labor. Aside from the fact he's French, I got the distinct impression he was up to no good. Oh, he seemed compliant enough, but he often appeared to be muttering something under his breath.

I actually caught him at it once. He must've thought the mic was off. I translated his comment, using my dog-eared French dictionary, as, "Die, English pig-dog!"

Julia managed to watch her back along with the béarnaise sauce and kept Jacques away from the cutlery as much as possible. She'll always be an idol of mine for her good taste, longevity, and her ability to work with practically anyone, including potentially homicidal Frenchmen.

Julia, *au revoir.*

Upward Mobility?

The worst part about living at home, of course, was the continual need to assert an adult personality in a household that still regarded me as a child—a big, hairy child, but a child nevertheless. I found myself slowly reverting to a state of retroactive puberty complete with adolescent mood swings, pimples, and excessive bad manners. My parents were not to blame, you understand, it was simply the situation. Predictably, the dam burst at one point, and I found it necessary, for the survival of both myself and my family, to move out.

> FREE ADVICE No. 6: Moving out of the house a second time can be even more traumatic for all concerned than the first. DON'T do it the way I did, *i.e.* sneak away in the dead of night while your parents are in California.

Having ventured out on my own—on my own actually being about six blocks away from my parents' house—my first difficulty was furniture. I didn't have any.

I was playing in a rock band at the time, and one of the guitar players had an old sofa bed he wanted to unload. He only lived about three blocks away, so we figured we could just schlep the thing down to my new basement apartment.

I should have known, when I first saw this monstrosity, that we were in for serious trouble. It was over six feet long and upholstered in that dingy beige shade so popular before color television. The works of the folding bed were iron—heavy, black iron—and the sharp ends of springs and suspenders poked out every which way.

Craig and I were used to hoisting heavy sound equipment around all the time, so we thought this would be a breeze. We found the sofa standing on end in the corner of a dark, filthy storage room in his apartment building and wrestled it to the ground.

We lugged it down the fire escape, dying a little at every step, and proceeded to Laurel-and-Hardy it down the street past two banks, a Methodist church, and the county mental health center. The proximity of the latter gave passing motorists a plausible explanation for the two longhaired hippy freaks sitting sprawled all over a thirty-year-old sofa bed in the middle of the street.

The easy part was installing it. We simply tipped it up on end and let it fall downstairs right through my front door.

FREE ADVICE No. 7: Used furniture is great, depending on how used it is, and who's been using it.

Several days of domesticity later, I found I had accumulated a large number of brown hard-shelled roommates. Roaches, formerly living in the stored couch, now found the time ripe for expansion. Soon they were eating my food, playing my records, and wearing my clothes.

This can happen to anyone. I once knew a piano teacher who bought a used baby grand, only to find that it came with its own babies. So always check for tiny livestock, and when in doubt, fumigate.

For the rest of my furnishings, I raided my parents' basement. So much for independence, but at least I had familiar things around me.

At this time, I was working at my first full-time job as a grade 5-12 band instructor. I taught everyone, beginners to jaded seniors. Now when I was applying for jobs, I had two criteria in mind: a reasonable chance for success, and a decent salary schedule. I should have realized the first of those wasn't going to pan out when the principal, at my interview, loosened his necktie, unbuttoned his cotton/polyester shirt, and showed me the scars from his quadruple bypass right out in the middle of the corridor.

Out of eighty-seven applications, I had eleven interviews and two job offers. The first was in a small town comfortably close to a large urban center, yet far enough away for safety. It was a nice facility with a good history and reputation. The other had all the same qualities, minus the good reputation, but the money was somewhat better. Plus, it was twelve miles from home.

"Aha!" I thought. "I could save a lot of money if I lived at home and commuted!" So went my logic, but if you were paying attention earlier, you have some idea of how *that* turned out.

The truth is, in the two and a half years I lived at home after college, I managed not to save a dime. In fact I was, and still am, in debt up to my ears. Why? Two words: Easy credit.

FREE ADVICE No. 8: Sometime during or after college you will be inundated with offers of pre-approved credit: Visa, MasterCard, Discover, American Express, what have you. *Do not take this as a tribute to your financial acumen!*

These companies are not handing you free money. Nor do they consider you, as a recent college graduate, to be a particularly good risk.

They consider you, as a recent college graduate, to be more stupid, naïve, and gullible than you ever were or will ever be again.

Think about it. Remember when you were on the playground, and your friend Billy offered to sell you his prize shooter, but you didn't have anything to swap for it? Billy said "Okay. How 'bout you give me a penny today, and a penny for every day you don't bring your marbles to trade. You get the boulder now, I get your marbles later, whaddya say?"

Did you agree? Of course not! Little kids are too shrewd for that. You knew damn well what that boulder was worth on the open market, and that your mom probably wouldn't let you bring your marbles to school anyway, and that soon Billy would be rolling in pennies while your pockets flapped in the breeze.

So now you've got your degree, and some bank in Maryland is offering you the keys to the kingdom for a low monthly payment at 18.5 percent APR. Are you going to walk away? Right, and I'm Smokey the Bear's gay brother Bob.

Whew, I'm getting a little worked up here. Better take a dinner break. Try this one on for size. It's not one of mine, actually. I got it from a telemarketer I got kind of chummy with once. She gave it to me over the phone after she talked me into taking out a five-year subscription to *Gullible* magazine, so I can't take "credit" for it.

Oops, sorry about that.

TURKEY LEG SOUP

Ingredients:

- 1 large turkey leg

- 1 medical prosthesis (for the turkey)

- 1 small bag egg noodles

- A couple of carrots, some celery, an onion, a bit o' bay leaf, a pinch of parsley

Directions:

- Place amputated leg in crock-pot and cover with water; add salt.

- Cook on high till the meat falls off the bone. (Sounds like the Donner Party, doesn't it?)

- Chop up veggies, once again, and add to pot. Add noodles.

- Cook till tender.

  This one comes highly recommended—by everyone but the turkey.

Working Man's Blues

Landing your first job is like losing your virginity, or vice-versa, depending on which order you do them in. But as wacky as my band students were most of the time, they were nothing compared to the hoops I had to jump through to get the gig in the first place.

Once I interviewed for an entire school board, the superintendent, and two building principals who looked like they'd just sat through the complete operas of Wagner's *Ring Cycle* one right after the other. Believe me, it's difficult to exude confidence when you're being interviewed by Mount Rushmore.

I drove two hours to get to that interview, and when I finally stood up and told them I wasn't interested in the job, they looked as relieved as I felt. I gathered I didn't make a good impression.

More often than not, though, I just talked to the principal. That was okay, except administrators are schooled in high-level diplomacy from birth so you never know quite where you stand. I had several interviews where the headman seemed to take an immediate shine to me—introduced me around, took me out to lunch, even showed me the locations of nice apartment buildings he thought might have a vacancy. Inevitably, I would come in second or third.

I'd get this sympathetic phone call from the guy that would go something like: "Jeff, I just wanted you to know that I was really pulling for you, but the board president's brother-in-law interviewed right after you did, and my hands were tied. I'm sure you understand. If there's ever anything I can do for you..."

Some of these jokers were so good I ended up apologizing to them for putting them in such an awkward position.

Probably the most unique interview I had was when I faced a panel of parents or "patrons" of the district—about a dozen and a half of them—each with his or her own pet theory of what constitutes a successful high school band program. The new owner of the local dry cleaners was especially profound. He waxed lyrical about how important marching band was to the community "at large"; how essential it was that all the music weenies hustle out on field every Friday night to wave the banner and beat the drum for the boys on the football team.

When he asked me my thoughts, I naturally gave the musician's point of view. The principal informed me that I'd probably blown it when I asked the gentleman pointedly what it was that *he* did for a living. What a feeling of satisfaction when I read that he had burned his own establishment to the ground in a freak crease-presser accident. Maybe he should have taken the band job.

My long-suffering parents bought me a new suit to interview in. By the time I finally got a job, that suit looked like Bogey's trench coat in that scene from *Casablanca* where Ingrid Bergman stands him up at the train station in the pouring rain. I had to take it in for a lube and oil change.

But, finally, I was an independent (sort of) professional (kind of) earning my own money (not really so much) and calling my own shots (for the most part). My first month as a band teacher was fascinating. I wore the obligatory huge wad of keys on my belt as a badge of office, and bore my older colleagues' patting me on the head and calling me "Junior G-man" as a sign of affection.

I soon began to learn the little quirks of adolescence—from the opposite point of view this time—and how to deal with them. Gradually I settled in to enjoy my chosen career. Then, suddenly, the reality of the situation struck me like the odor of a flatulent camel: My First Paycheck.

Withholding? What's withholding? Nobody told me they would actually *withhold* part of my pay! What for? What had I done? Wait a minute. FED? FICA? *Who are they and what have they done with my money?*

I went to the business office and slowly sank to the floor as the secretary calmly and patiently explained to me the fiscal facts of life. My spirit nearly broke as the dear lady, with grandmotherly sympathy, pointed out what the notations on my pay stub meant (appropriate word, "stub"), and I went back to my office sadder, but wiser.

By the end of the day, however, my mood was much lighter, realizing that (a) I had no rent to pay (yet), as I was still living at home at the time, (b) I had no debt (yet) outside of about $15,000 in student loans, and (c) I still had close to a thousand bucks to stick in the bank that Uncle Sam and the great state of Iowa had graciously allowed me to keep. This was the stuff dreams are made on (Bogey again).

My friend Craig—yes, the guy with the roach-ridden sofa bed—was what you would call your basic audiophile. He would opt not to eat for months at a time in order to afford a new piece of stereo equipment. Unfortunately, I caught that bug from him, too.

The first thing I bought was Craig's classic German turntable and cartridge. The thing was priceless, but he needed money for a new custom guitar so I got a pretty good deal. Then, of course, I had to have the receiver, speakers, custom speaker stands and extruded, copper-alloy, gold-tipped connecting cables to go with it. Before I was through, I had close to a year's salary tied up in high-end audio, and it wasn't even Christmas.

FREE ADVICE No. 9: Better to throw your money down a dry hole than try to keep up with the Joneses. Particularly if the Joneses are insane.

As brevity is the soul of wit, we shall now skip lightly over some fascinating autobiographical detail, not only for the sake of time, but also, frankly, because it was a most embarrassing period in my life. I'm afraid if I start thinking about it I'll end up sticking my fingers in my ears and chanting "la la la" until it all goes away.

Anyway, what's the point of showing myself up to be a chump at this stage of the game? It'll just ruin the rest of the book for you, and we certainly don't want that. Let's just move on with my credibility intact, shall we? It'll be much better for both of us, I promise.

You'll get much of the flavor of the period, however, from my next recipe:

KAMAKAZE DEATH-DOGS

Ingredients:

- 1 pkg. wieners

- Several slices American cheese

- 1 small jar picante sauce or salsa

- Chopped onions

- Sauerkraut

- Bread or hotdog buns

Directions:

- Slice wienies lengthwise; lay diagonally across bread slices

- Cover with small slices of cheese.

- Pour on salsa or picante.

- Add kraut to taste.

- Nuke 'em for about 1 min. per dog.

- Top with chopped onions and your favorite condiments. (Get your mind out of the gutter!)

- Belch.

Okay, so this one isn't particularly elegant, but it's a good one to try when you need comfort food or are feeling self-abusive.

Love Conquers

In my second year of teaching, I met a woman. Hair red as flame, she had. I noticed that striking head of hair immediately because the first time we met, it was moussed down into a shiny orange helmet. Her hair on that day could have stood up to gale force winds. Little did I know that this was my future bride-to-be.

Even littler did I know that a dear friend of mine had cooked up this "accidental" meeting, having arranged it such that I had no choice but to sit next to her in his passenger van as he chauffeured a number of us young educators to a meeting. I've forgiven him by now, of course. Still, I'd have avoided a great deal of agony—and some occasional ecstasy—had I gone with my gut reaction.

FREE ADVICE No. 10: Always go with your first impression. If the milk's sour when you open the carton, it won't get any sweeter with time. THROW IT OUT!

I hardly saw this chick for months after that, but she called me the following summer, completely out of the blue, ostensibly for some sage wisdom on how to handle baton-twirlers. Turned out she was teaching at a competing school just a few miles away. I pontificated loud and long, never letting on that my own color guard looked like a platoon of amputees trying to perform close-order drill.

We made a date. I took her to my favorite Irish bar. Someone had apparently clued her in about the styling mousse because she'd dispensed with the helmet and let her coppery curls fall softly over her shoulders. She looked pretty spiffy, as a matter of fact. And so did I.

No, really! I hadn't had an actual date in donkey's years and I went all out for this one—showering every hour on the hour and rehearsing suave opening lines and witheringly sexy facial expressions in front of the bathroom mirror all day long.

God! If only I'd made some stupid, sexist comment or spilled cold beer in her lap, but no. I had to pick that night to be perfectly charming, considerate, and sexy. By midnight, I was a dead duck.

I had one more chance to escape fate when I took her home, by which time it was apparent that she hadn't had a date in a while, either. I had a pretty good idea that the evening did not necessarily have to end at her front door, but I muffed it again and decided to play the perfect gentleman. In fact, I didn't even kiss her till our fourth or fifth date. Girls are nuts about a guy with self-restraint. Intrigued by the novelty, I suppose.

FREE ADVICE No.11: I'm going to put forth a radical idea here, so bear with me. Always wait for the woman to make the first move.

I have used the frustration factor to my advantage as a matter of policy most of my life. It requires infinite patience but has never failed me yet. Of course, I am reasonably attractive. At the end of the evening of our fifth or sixth time out she asked me to, if I wanted to, "come in for awhile"—pointedly and with emphasis. As soon as the door closed, Doris grabbed me by the ears and hit me with a kiss that knocked me into geosynchronous orbit. This impressed me very much.

Now, I should have noticed some things about her right away. Of course, I was otherwise occupied at the time, but the first thing I should have noticed was her cat. Great cat. Liked to sneak up and bite me in the ass while my attention was elsewhere. The second thing I should have noticed was the cat's litter box. It was overflowing. Either the little guy was a really big eater, or the woman never—ever—cleaned it out.

She appeared to be quite the little pack rat as well. She had garage-sale furniture even worse than mine that the cat used as scratching posts—make that *gouging* posts.

Her closets and other storage spaces were a study in potential energy—a dam waiting to burst. The woman had more clothes than I'd had hot dinners, and she apparently never threw anything away.

Now, I'm not completely anal, but I do prefer carpet to kitty litter under my feet when I go to the bathroom at night, and I enjoy a certain harmony and logic in my closets. Why these observations didn't trigger some sort of immediate negative response, I don't know. I never commented, never complained, but often I'd scoop out the litter box and put the waste in a trash bag while Doris was out of the room.

Our relationship progressed as I continued to overlook one glaring warning sign after another. One New Year's Eve, I played a gig in a nearby town following a delicious but tense dinner with my parents and my beloved. Ten minutes after leaving the restaurant, I slid on a patch of black ice and rolled my car into a ditch. Three days later, while my vehicle was being repaired, I hit a deer broadside with a rental car while on my way to see Doris to apologize for leaving her with my parents on New Year's. A sign from the Almighty? You tell me.

I cooked my first dinner for Doris very soon after. Cooking an elegant dinner for a woman almost always impresses the hell out of her. It's also a great way to make amends for any stupid *faux pas* you might commit, like leaving her with your parents on a holiday. (Should that have been FREE ADVICE No. 12? Oh well, too late now.)

Here's what I cooked for her:

BONELESS, BRAINLESS CHICKEN DIJON

Ingredients:

- 4 boneless breast fillets (Get your mind out of the gutter again!)

- Light salad dressing or mayonnaise

- Creamy horseradish sauce

- Dijon mustard

Instructions:

- Spray a large, flat baking pan (Pyrex is good. That's the clear, glassy stuff.) with cooking spray.

- Lay out the breasts (Dammit, quit snickering!) in the pan.

- Mix salad dressing, mustard and horseradish to taste in a bowl. The proportions are up to you, but use more dressing than mustard, and more mustard than horseradish.

- Brush mixture over chicken.

- Bake at 350 for at least a half hour and no more than 45 mins. The mixture should form a light, golden-brown crust like a gypsy moth cocoon.

Strange Attractors

Doris had a thing about shoulder pads. You know, those pointy foam-rubber things women wear under a dress or blouse to get that stern, angular power-look so appropriate for home or office? The first time one of them came loose in the dryer, I brought it to her with a sad, sympathetic look on my face saying, "Sweetie, you don't need these. I love you just the way you are. You know what they say: more than a handful's just a waste."

She explained to me, in no uncertain terms, that these were for her *shoulders*.

I first lost my mind and told her I loved her in the backseat of our friend Dee's Mazda on the way home from a road-trip to Omaha. I meant it, too. Really. Somehow, though, I just can't seem to recapture the passion of that moment. It's like it all happened to someone else.

Would t'were it had.

You have by now sensed where this is heading. We are moving now into that brief period in which I was no longer a WASPB, but had, in fact, become a WASPMP (White Anglo-Saxon Protestant Married Person). Although this may seem to waver outside our original mission, I feel it will be instructive. And, since this period was so brief, the bloom was barely off my bachelorhood when it was suddenly restored to me. But we have to go through this to get to that, if you see what I mean.

Doris' apartment was in the neighboring town where she taught. It was in a horrible old building owned by the school district and popularly known as "The Teacherage." She became uncomfortable living under the eyes of the local townspeople, whom she regarded as "snoopy," and our relationship had matured to the point where she and I enjoyed closer proximity. Often as close as humanly possible.

So Doris took a marginally better place near mine in my hometown. In fact, it was in convenient walking distance from my basement digs. For most of the next year, we officially maintained separate addresses while, in actuality, we had set up housekeeping together, alternating evenings between my house and hers. Monday, Wednesday, Friday and every other Sunday we slept in the fold-up former cockroach residence in my living room; Tuesday, Thursday, Saturday and alternate Sundays, on her floor in sleeping bags. Well, it wasn't quite that regular, but you get the idea.

I was always a little nervous staying at her place. For one thing, the clutter drove me crazy. For another, I always had to keep an eye out for the cat. Also, the wiring was terrible. I don't know how many blow dryers we burned out in the eighteen or so months of our engagement, but Doris' hair, as I recall, got progressively frizzier. I began to be nostalgic for the shiny orange helmet.

I'm not sure whether Doris and my family took an instant dislike to each other, or if it happened gradually over time. Either way, it was obvious from the start that I had a real selling job to do on both of them.

You see, I belong to one of those oddities of modern life—a close family. I know the names of all my relatives—most of whom live within a hundred miles of each other—see them regularly, and like a considerable portion of them. Doris' family is similar in that they are pretty much concentrated in a small geographic area. Beyond that, however, they can only be described as "close" in terms of friction.

FREE ADVICE No. 12: All that stuff you've been told about checking out the mother, because that's what the daughter will be like in thirty years—IT'S TRUE!

I was present when Doris and her mom stuffed her World War II veteran father into a nursing home kicking and screaming. They said it was senile dementia, but I think they just didn't like him. It scared the hell out of me.

Remember, you're not just marrying a girl. You're marrying a family with its own prevailing culture. In a sense, every marriage is a mixed marriage, and opposites, while they do attract, also tend to violently cancel each other out.

Doris' main objection seemed to be that I spent too much time with my family. Too much for what, I'm not sure. But she was right in the sense that I stopped in at my folks' house at least once a day, since Mom was alone in the house a lot due to my father's long commute, and she often needed help managing a small acreage and a kennel full of large, rambunctious puppy dogs left over from my school days.

On the other hand, my parents' problem with my beloved seemed to have had more to do with her general attitude and outlook, neither of which I could do anything about. She hated small-town life, and dreamed of the day when, instead of being a mere high school band director in Shelby, Iowa, she would become a mere high school band director in Des Moines, Iowa. The rural-ness of many of my friends and relations annoyed her, and any attempt to welcome her into the family met with cold toleration at best; outright sneering contempt at worst.

You can imagine that I was under considerable emotional stress at this time. I believe this is when I really began to enjoy cooking. Unfortunately, I also started to enjoy eating and drinking more and more. Consequently, I grew to resemble that famous children's character of A.A. Milne, causing my significant other to issue me the pet name "Pooh." One of my favorite concoctions from this period I call:

FLAMETHROWER CHILI

Ingredients:

- 1 lb. hamburger

- 1 lg. onion

- 1 can whole tomatoes

- 1 can tomato sauce

- 1 can tomato paste

- 2 cans red chili beans

- ½ lb. or so jalapeno peppers

- Cajun or Creole spice or ground cayenne pepper

- Several pitchers of ice-water

Directions:

- Brown hamburger and drain.

- Fill sink; slice onions underwater (a trick I forgot to tell you about earlier).

- Open all cans; dump into crock-pot; add hamburger, onions.

- While slow cooker warms up, slice jalapenos (definitely underwater!) into relatively thin slices. Use a sharp, serrated knife, otherwise you'll have tiny jalapeno seeds squirting out all over the place, and who needs that? Add to chili.

- Let the stuff cook for a good, long while. Have ice water handy when you taste-test it. You may find that you need to pour some straight into the soup. Or you may need to add cayenne and/or Cajun spice and/or regular chili powder to fire it up a little.

- Hint: If your eyeballs don't sweat, it ain't hot enough.

You may have noticed a much more businesslike tone to this recipe. This is because some of the ingredients are very dangerous and must be treated with respect. One of the cooks at my school was out for three weeks with second-degree burns on both hands from putting up her own homemade salsa. Not too shrewd, considering her sister in New Mexico had shipped the peppers in an asbestos packing crate. On the other hand, it does have the effect of taking your mind completely off your troubles for a while.

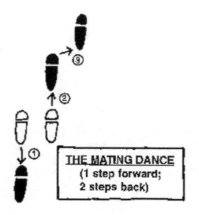

THE MATING DANCE
(1 step forward;
2 steps back)

The Mating Dance

The band I used to play in frequented crummy little outhouse bars in small Iowa towns. We had a dedicated following of illiterates, despite the fact that we tried to slick up our act too much for their taste by employing well-rehearsed, four-part harmony and songs by J.J. Cale.

Of course, to prevent death by flying beer bottle, we had to do at least one country set per night. This was back when country was still country. Nowadays, the only way you can tell a country band from a rock group is by their big-ass hats.

Our bass player heard about a country-western "battle of the bands" contest being held nearby, and we decided to enter. I invited Doris along, and she and I and Craig crammed all our gear into my little Mazda GLC.

We were a big hit. There must've been five or six hundred suburban cowboys packed into this tiny hotel "ballroom." Most of the other acts were of the twangy, jug-band variety—strictly amateurs. We threw in a little Elvis with our Oak Ridge Boys, and the crowd went wild.

High on beer and adulation, I proposed to Doris in the parking lot, while several Willie Nelson wannabes puked their guts out behind an overflowing dumpster. Moonlight cast a pearly glow over it all. We kissed breathlessly. Her eyes were moist and dewy. My nose was running from hay fever.

It was a magical night.

We kept our engagement secret for a time. Things were already pretty tense, and I had begun to spend less and less time with my family, which, of course, made Doris very happy. We resolved to wait for the proper moment.

We thought the moment had come when my parents invited both of us to accompany them to Minnesota for the annual family fishing trip. I was excited. I knew in my heart that in the beautiful "Land of 10,000 Lakes," amidst the peace of nature and the sound of rippling water, we'd all get to know each other better and live happily ever after.

Ever been broken on the rack? I now know what it feels like—very similar to going on vacation with your folks and your fiancée. I didn't consciously realize that my family had only agreed to tolerate Doris for my sake—a noble parental attitude—or that she'd agreed to go only because she knew how important it was to me, which was also pretty nice, come to think of it. And me? Well, of course I didn't even *think* of simply dragging everything out into the open. I just did this marvelous emotional juggling act, trying to keep my balls in the air, so to speak.

FREE ADVICE No. 13: I still have problems with this one, but please have the *cojones* to tell your loved ones exactly how you feel, what you're doing with your life, what the hell's wrong with you, etc. DON'T BE SUCH A WUSS!

It will be uncomfortable, at times, but not as uncomfortable as trying to please all the people all the time, and feeling continuously wretched.

Remember, if your parents hadn't intended you to grow up and be a man, they'd have had a girl.

My beloved definitely helped matters along by constantly bitching about everything from the condition of the cabins to the temperature of the water in the lake. The folks, for their part, were unhappy with our public displays of affection, which my mother claimed amounted to foreplay on the beach. Things were, as they say, a mess.

We were playing a board game one rainy day, and proceeded to get into an argument over the rules and over Doris' contention that my mother's typically pithy comments were aimed at her, which some of them probably were. The discussion turned abruptly to whether Doris and I had made any definite plans—and the cat was suddenly out of the bag. Fortunately, most of the denouement has fled from my memory, but I'm sure it was quite unpleasant.

The next several months were a study in grim responsibility, with my parents dutifully inviting us over for dinner every Sunday night, and me talking Doris into accepting once in a while. Doris threw some of her more memorable tantrums after those dinners, and there were several occasions where we heaved the rings at one another. Somehow, though, we always seemed to find them back on our fingers a day or two later. Don't ask me why.

The funny thing is, as badly as Doris and my family got along, I was a big, big hit with hers. Honestly, they loved me—at least I'm pretty sure they did.

On the other hand, in all the trips we made across the state to visit them, I never once stayed at her parents' house. I always ended up sleeping on the living room floor at her brother's. He had a wife, four kids, a flatulent dog, and virtually no room to spare, while the ancestral manse was a rambling three-story brick affair, which, admittedly, had seen better days, but you could put a visiting rugby team up in the place and never see hide nor hair of anybody for a week.

Still, I slept on the floor at the brother's. Go figure.

I found out some interesting things about my incipient in-laws on these trips. For instance, there appeared to be a history of mental instability in the family, beginning with an "Uncle Pinky," whom I don't believe I ever met. If I had met an "Uncle Pinky," I think I would remember. And I kept hearing things from them like, "Oh, you're so *good* for Doris! We've never seen her so relaxed."

I think I must have had some inkling of what was to come because I kept dragging my feet on the wedding plans. So Doris made the plans and I wrote the checks. Her family supposedly couldn't afford to put on a wedding, and I sure as hell wasn't going to ask my folks to shell out, so we paid for most of it ourselves.

Doris' mom did do some of the legwork, though. At one time she made arrangements to hold the reception in the basement of a bowling alley. I put my foot down, which is the only assertive thing I can recall doing at the time.

What was holding us together, at this point, I honestly don't know. Sex was a biggie. We were both very passionate people, and Doris had a pretty good imagination, though very little opportunity to exercise it before I came along. Outside of that, we had very little in common.

I'm a night owl by nature. Doris crashed pretty regularly about nine p.m. I loved M*A*S*H reruns, while her idea of good TV was *Who's the Boss*. We were just two different people, to coin a cliché.

Often, Doris would fall asleep next to me on the sofa bed. It was then that I enjoyed some quiet time and flipped the remote at will. I'd slip quietly into the kitchen and make myself a special snack, just to pretend I was still footloose and fancy-free. Usually it was an entire eight-pack of hot dogs, but sometimes I'd get creative.

Here's what I'd fix:

ANY PORT IN A STORM PIZZA

Ingredients:

* 1 pkg. English muffins

* 1 jar prepared spaghetti sauce

* Whatever else you've got

Directions:

* Slice muffins in half horizontally (side-to-side).

* Cover muffins with sauce using spoon or basting brush.

* Put W.E.Y.G. (ingredient 3) on top. I've used lunchmeat, stew meat, bacon, broccoli, American cheese, cottage cheese, ricotta cheese, headcheese, cocktail olives, pickled beets...Use your imagination.

* Place under broiler on a cookie sheet till toppings melt, or in the microwave till the glass door steams over.

Glorious!

Conscientious Objector

I know what you're saying. You're saying, "So you got yourself into a bad situation. Why didn't you just walk away? Be a man, for chrissake!"

Well, the truth is I thought I was. I mean, I was the one who proposed. A man's gotta keep his commitments, doesn't he? Well, *doesn't he?*

That was pretty much the way my mind worked then. There were so many times when I just wanted to chuck the whole kit'n caboodle, but I didn't. Why? I'll say it softly.

(I was in love.)

Oh yeah, the real thing—skyrockets and all. Of course, I wasn't even sure I *liked* the girl half the time, but I was quite sure I was in love with her, and neither my well-meaning family nor my friends were able to talk me out of it. Believe me, they tried.

Not to say that I was precisely a prince. Far from it. I was passive/
aggressive about the wedding plans, positively anal about forcing everybody to get along whether they wanted to or not, and paranoid as hell
about everything and everyone around me. Doris wasn't having a particularly good time either.

As the last few weeks before the wedding dragged on, we "took
instruction" from this Lutheran minister in Doris' hometown. Now,
Doris wasn't terribly religious, and I'm really only a Protestant by
upbringing. Apparently, girls are the only things I'm *not* appropriately
skeptical about. As far as I could tell, she had no connection to this
church at all and had simply picked it out at random.

Of course, I'd never been there before in my life, so the whole thing
seemed an incredible sham. The minister, however, was terrific. I only
wish I'd paid closer attention to him.

He gave us these very charming compatibility tests with questions
like: "How important do you consider sexual compatibility to be within
the context of marriage—not important, somewhat important, moderately important, or *extremely* important?" Pretty hip for a religious quiz.

Later, we'd talk out the results and their ramifications for the success
of our marriage. We had several sessions over a period of five or six
weeks. At the end of it all, I'm quite certain the good reverend's personal opinion was that not only should we *not* get married, but the two
of us shouldn't even live in the same hemisphere if we could possibly
help it.

Of course, what he said was something like, "Your love for each
other will sustain you through the storms that lie ahead." Wimp.

Oh, I don't really blame him. After all, the man had a wife and kids,
and fifty bucks is fifty bucks, right?

My family and hers had never met, except that one time Doris
brought her mother over for one of our big Easter feeds at my parents'
house. It was pleasant enough, but a return invitation just never seemed
in the offing. Just a few weeks before the wedding, my soon-to-be
mom-in-law said, "Oh, you must have your lovely family come out and
OK all the arrangements I've made."

I've made? Ha! Doris did most of it herself with me dragging my feet behind her and her mother occupying the in-law seat in the back of the car.

My folks, my sister, and my grandmother drove three hundred miles expecting to stay overnight. We ended up meeting in a yogurt joint, touring the church and the reception hall (fortunately not the bowling alley, or my mother would have had a stroke), and then parting company. Not even a dinner invitation. I stayed at Doris' brother's that night, as usual, and slept on the floor with Beatrice, the dog, embarrassed to tears.

And still I went through with it. Most of my relatives were too old to make the trip, and most of my friends were involved in the wedding—the whole affair having expanded to five bridesmaids, five groomsmen, two sets of musicians and various and sundry side boys and handmaidens—so the groom's side of the aisle was quite sparse. The mood was grim. My folks wandered around before the ceremony looking like victims of real-estate fraud. My friends all got drunk in my honor, telling my family what a mistake they thought I was making. My best man—who I now suspect is sleeping with my ex, poor sap—left a fifth of Scotch in the clothes bag my tux came in, and I sneaked several nips from it before the ceremony to get my gumption up. I remember my mom, wearing the face she reserves for funerals, hugging me tight two minutes before zero hour, and asking me tenderly if I was happy, making it clear that she'd never believe me even if I said I was.

On top of everything else, I had planned to sing.

FREE ADVICE No. 14: Do not sing, play a musical instrument, juggle, or otherwise perform at your own wedding, or any other solemn occasion in which you yourself figure prominently.

I sleepwalked through most of the ceremony, didn't notice Doris stalk down the aisle, didn't even see her best friend's father with the enormous, obsolete video camera trying hard to be inconspicuous as he aimed it over the minister's shoulder. I came to consciousness just in time for the "special music from the groom to his bride."

I'd picked out a Stevie Wonder tune that was way too high for me, especially in my present stressful state. The fact that my rental tuxedo pants didn't fit particularly well should have helped, theoretically, but didn't. The title was "Overjoyed," which, to be honest, I wasn't. I was stiff, scared, tongue-tied and to top it all off, I was pretty sure I felt something inside of me tear open when I failed to hit the high F-sharp at the end.

I felt better about things the more I gazed at my bride in that creamy white dress. She looked really, really beautiful. Her hair was like spun gold in the light of the candles. Her eyes sparkled through joyful tears.

Of course, a lady rhino looks good on her wedding day.

The ceremony was mercifully brief, but the shower of rice at the end seemed half-hearted at best. The rice, you know, is a fertility ritual. I suppose the idea of the two of us breeding was too horrible to contemplate.

When my best man started the car to take us to the reception, my only comment was "Let's go, I'm hungry." Really, it's on the videotape and everything.

The restaurant was one of those warehouse places that trades on the bar and the atmosphere as much as the food. The reception area was in a kind of loft, which was really rather quaint. I finally relaxed when our guests began to mill around and socialize, waiting for dinner to start.

Now Doris had lectured me loud and long on several occasions not to moosh the wedding cake in her face when we posed for the obligatory cake-slicing picture. Apparently, she'd been to several weddings where the Neanderthal groom had mooshed the cake all over the bride's face just at the point where the camera flashed. I couldn't figure out why she seemed to think *I* was the type of guy who would moosh the cake all over the bride's face just at the point where the camera flashed, but apparently she did. I was so sick of hearing about it that I actually contemplated mooshing the cake all over the bride's face just at the point where the camera flashed.

I thought about it, but I didn't do it.

We had a disc jockey and a dance floor, but nobody seemed in much of a mood to boogie. There was an air of forced gaiety about the whole affair that Doris and I and both our families did our best to encourage. Her father, however, was crying throughout most of the reception. My grandmother told me much later that she was pretty sure he was crying for me.

For those of you who want to start cooking for yourselves, but are afraid to look wimpy, you could start with barbecuing. Searing raw, red meat over an open flame is about as macho as you can get. Since I'm feeling rather vulnerable right now, here's my very own barbecue sauce recipe:

MACHO BARBECUE SAUCE

Ingredients:

- 2 cups catsup or bottled barbecue sauce if you're unsure of yourself

- ¼ lb. butter or margarine

- ½ cup Worcestershire sauce

- ½ cup honey

- onion powder, garlic powder, chili powder, talcum powder (barbecuing is hot work!)

- 1 twelve-pack premium beer

Directions:

- In the oldest, crustiest saucepan you've got, melt butter over hot coals (on the grill). Add catsup, ketchup or barbecue sauce.

- Blend in Worcestershire sauce and honey.

- Add seasonings to taste.

- Bring sauce to a light boil, stirring a lot.

- When sauce just begins to bubble, add beer a dollop at a time. Alternate dollops between the sauce, yourself, and your friends for proper timing: A dollop for you, a dollop for the sauce, a dollop for you, a dollop for your buddy, etc. That way, neither you nor the sauce will be overwhelmed, and you're more likely to remember to put the meat on.

Notice we're using more or less precise measurements on this one. Barbecue sauce is much like high school chemistry: One false move and you'll blow the whole thing to hell.

Marital Bliss

Don't worry. This will be a very short chapter.

We spent the night in a motel in town. Suffice it to say that, after the stress of the ceremony and its aftermath, we were both relieved to have it over with, and our wedding night proceeded as wedding nights do. (You want play-by-play, tune in ESPN.)

The next morning, my mother-in-law hosted a brunch in our honor, held, naturally, at Doris' brother's. Everybody who attended the wedding was invited including, surprisingly enough, my family.

The little house was stuffed with well-wishers bearing gifts. I was entirely uncomfortable with the idea of opening all those presents in front of God and everyone. I mean, what if I opened something so incredibly tacky that I couldn't even fain appreciation? But by that time, I was so used to discomfort that I pulled it off fairly well. Doris even said so.

They sat us down in the living room on thrones made of dinette chairs covered with sheets and crepe paper, and made a big fat hairy deal about handing us the gifts one by one, and having each respective donor come forward to snap a picture as we ceremoniously opened them. After the fourth shadow-box wall clock, it was difficult to ooh and ahh convincingly.

The highlight of the morning was the food. The main course was a remarkable egg casserole for which I, unfortunately, never got the recipe. I was very impressed because in all the time I spent with Doris' family, I had never, ever tasted her mother's cooking as far as I knew.

It turned out I wasn't tasting it then, either. My new sister-in-law, Liz, the lady of the house and, for all intents and purposes, the matriarch of the family, had prepared everything and purchased all the ingredients.

I must say a quick word about my former in-laws. After all these years, I still think fondly about Liz and her kids. Doris' brother was nice enough, but as far as I could tell, the extent to which he involved himself in family matters taking place more than four feet away from his Barcalounger was somewhere in the vicinity of diddly-squat.

No, that's not fair. It wasn't diddly-squat. It was more like what diddly-squat does in its spare time.

Liz, on the other hand, was a terrific wife and mother despite holding down a full time nursing job. She always did her best to make me feel welcome and part of the family, and was quite honest with me about what she thought I was getting myself into. Even though her loyalties must necessarily lie with my ex, I have a sneaking hunch she will sympathize with this when she reads it. Although, classy lady that she is, she will never say so.

Maybe I should have married her instead.

Doris and I honeymooned in a ski resort. We had a beautiful suite complete with authentic antique furniture, a Jacuzzi in the bathroom and complementary champagne on ice when we arrived. The resort's mascot was a huge English mastiff named Bear, who immediately became our best friend. It was absolutely perfect, even off-season.

For three blissful days, we achieved a flawless communion of souls. We were entirely in tune, one with the other, each of us attaining greatest happiness in pleasing the other.

And then it was time to go home.

I met a graduate student from England the other night who shared with me a quick way to fix scrambled eggs without a skillet or stove. I wish I'd met him before my honeymoon, as I was in no mood to cook breakfast the day after.

If you have a microwave and a glass bowl, try this:

NICK'S PICADILLY SCRAMBLED EGGS

Ingredients:

- Eggs

- Link sausage (bangers, for you Anglophiles)

- Onions, peppers, salt, black pepper, etc.

Directions:

- Slice up your "bangers," and chop up your veggies.

- Break eggs into bowl; add other stuff.

- Microwave on high about 30 secs. at a time until eggs begin to cook at the edges and then stir the more solid bits toward the center. Keep cooking in annoying, 30-second installments until done.

I must tell you this fellow is a rugby player, so I can't guarantee this recipe isn't the result of severe head trauma. On the other hand, if you want scrambled eggs and all you've got to work with is a microwave, your options are pretty limited.

Cheerio, lads!

Hearth and Home

When we got home from our three days in paradise, we were faced with many choices. The first of which was: "Your place or mine?"

My apartment was mostly below ground, with a single tiny bedroom. Hers, as I said, was a two-bedroom firetrap. I persuaded her that we could put up with subterranean life for a year or so, and thereby save up for a place with a slightly better view. Plus my place had been recently remodeled, so it looked pretty nice. It was two steps from the laundry room, and we never had to worry about tornadoes.

What I failed to anticipate was how painful it would be to turn my place into our place. Though Doris had occupied it with me on and off for almost two years, my little hole in the ground had been my sanctuary, my stronghold. Suddenly, down came my six-foot rattan wall hanging of W.C. Fields, thumbs on lapels, quipping his famous quip, "Any man who hates dogs and children can't be all bad," and up went a whole lot of cross-stitched kittens. Down came my giant Bogey poster, and up went hearts and flowers. I was in shock.

I was a sport about it, though. I banged in all the nails.

We also suffered a pronounced lack of closet space. My bride, on the other hand, suffered no lack of clothes. Late-night TV came to our rescue, however, and soon in the mail came a crate full of "Closet Savers."

I neglected to mention that during our courtship, I had become a cat-owner. Now, I was raised by dog-people, and cats are entirely unheard of in my upbringing. I am also moderately allergic to cats. Simply petting a Persian can send me into spasms. But Doris positively doted on her little Andy, and just to impress her, I came home from the mall one day with an adorable gray tabby I named Katy. Katy the kitty. Kate the cat.

I grew really fond of the little fur-ball. For the first week or so she ate her fuzzy little head off, and then, after a meal, would leap into my lap, rub my chest, buzz, curl up, and fall cutely asleep. Katy did all the usual tricks with yarn and kitty-toys—I got her the little rubber mousie with the bell inside, the bag full of catnip, the whole works—and she had a knack for stealing small shiny objects, like watches and jewelry, and hiding them where I wouldn't find them for weeks.

Then she got sick, stopped eating altogether, and began to vomit a lot. This went on for about two months, after which she finally went off the starvation diet with a vengeance. Katy now weighs about thirty-two pounds, and holds down the same two square feet of floor space in my ex's apartment on a permanent basis.

When Katy first adopted me, the only logical place to put her litter box was in the very short hallway to the bathroom. When Doris and Andy, the ferocious butt-biter, moved in, we learned that two cats who were not raised together will not use the same litter box. So now we had not one, but two feline waste-disposal units lying open to the air between the kitchen and the lavatory. Not a good situation odor-wise, and the tendency to step barefoot in kitty litter and other disgusting substances in the middle of the night was very grave.

As my furniture was marginally better, we sold or discarded most of hers. Andy's scratching-post couch went, cockroach heaven stayed, as did Doris' two behemoth chests of drawers, which we had to stack one on top of the other in the bedroom. We nailed some shelving up in the bathroom for all her makeup and stuff, and coats and vacuum cleaner attachments went in the same microscopic closet with towels and bed linens. We were what you might call cramped.

> FREE ADVICE No. 15: In a marriage or any other cohabitation arrangement, your serenity index will be directly proportional to the amount of available storage space. Stash your stuff under the bed or in the trunk of your car if you have to. It's worth it.

Unfortunately, we had no bed yet. I had been sleeping in the tiny twin bed I'd had since I was three years old. That obviously wouldn't do, so back it went to my parent's basement. For the first few weeks, Doris and I slept in cockroach heaven, hoping and praying every night that when we woke up, it would be just the two of us—or just the four of us, if you count the kitties. We had a little wedding money left, so one weekend we went bed shopping. It was then I learned my beloved spouse had Cadillac tastes on a Yugo salary.

Now, to me, a bed is simply a place to sleep, and to strengthen the bonds of a blossoming relationship. As picky as she was, you'd have thought we were picking out a sarcophagus for King Tut. We must have spent nine hours shopping just for the headboard.

Finally we found something she could live with that was in shouting distance of our price range. We got a nice mock brass job on sale for about ninety-nine bucks complete with frame. I was happy, and Doris seemed content.

Then it was mattress time. There was a factory outlet in the mall, and we had a good time playing "Princess and the Pea" all over the store. Actually, it was more like "Goldilocks"—"This one's too hard, this one's too soft..." You get the idea.

Well, we found out you can't get much in the way of a mattress and box spring for less than three hundred dollars. We had to settle for something other than the Deluxe Posture Perfect Sleeper Supreme, which was our first choice. Doris was disappointed, but agreed that anything was better than the Cockroach Hilton, which was, at that very moment, stuck at half-mast in our living room.

With our new workbench properly installed, we began to build our new life together. We should have called in a professional contractor.

Strangely enough, one thing we were short of was cooking utensils. I had to improvise, making various culinary vessels, devices, and appliances do things they were never brought up to do. Hence, the next recipe:

WOK-DOGS

Ingredients:

- 1 pkg. wienies

- 1 can of beer

- 1 wire steaming rack or circular spatter-screen

- 1 wok (a real one, not one of those non-stick electric jobs)

Directions:

- Empty beer into wok. (I know it seems like a waste, but trust me.)

- Place steamer or spatter-screen in wok over the beer.

- Put wienies on steamer or screen.

- Turn stove on high and steam until done.

This is a concept that works with many kinds of meat. I like to steam the excess fat off of a rack of ribs before grilling. The beer gives a great flavor, and you can have lots of fun surveying beers for taste and bouquet!

Beginning of the End

Our life together, unfortunately, was dominated by our work. Sociologists tell us not to look for mates in the workplace—that it can give rise to all kinds of professional jealousy and political intrigue. I knew all this, but technically Doris and I didn't work together so I thought we'd sort of, you know, squeak by.

We did share a career, however, which is not so bad in itself, but in competing institutions, it can get rather hairy. Particularly so in our case because she was so much better at it than I was. No, strike that. Let's just say she was a lot more *intense*.

I always got home from work first, homebody that I am. I'd open up a beer, turn on the stereo, and happily begin preparing supper. Then Doris would come in, immediately turn off the stereo, and proceed to relate all the petty frustrations of her day, vigorously and emotionally, standing less than a foot away and slowly backing me up against the countertop. She'd pour out her enmity toward her principal, her pupils, and their parents, all the while making these terribly aggressive slashing motions with her hand, never seeming to realize that I had suffered the very same indignities not twenty miles away at the very same time, and had come home to forget them.

I'd nod and try to look sympathetic, feeling my personal space being rudely violated by my own spouse. I felt terribly put-upon, especially since I had already cleaned out both cat-boxes and started dinner—even washed my hands in between. I felt I deserved better treatment.

But I had read all about this deep-seated need women have to talk out their day, and I was trying to be an understanding hubby, if there really is such a thing. Consequently, I took to smiling and murmuring, "Yes, darling. I know, sweetheart," a lot.

I didn't complain because I honestly felt that our real communication took place in other ways. And boy, did we communicate sometimes! That is, until the differences in our circadian rhythms became apparent.

Very often, I'd feel Doris snuggling up to me in my sleep. I'd crack my eyelids open and peek at the bedside clock. It was usually somewhere between five and six in the morning. My God! I couldn't even work up an erotic dream at that ghastly cow-milking hour.

I'm a night person. Anywhere between eleven at night and two-thirty in the morning. would have been ideal for me, and sometimes was, although Doris tended to fall asleep in the middle. Very demoralizing.

Weekends were our saving grace. Having that time together kept us from being at each other's throats the rest of the week, as long as I didn't interrupt her afternoon nap. We were well rested and eager, with plenty of time on our hands. Unfortunately, you can't hold a relationship together by sex alone, though we certainly gave it the old college try.

It was money that proved the ultimate vehicle of our destruction. Now admittedly, I am not the world's foremost authority on personal finance, but at least I record most of the checks I write. Maybe not right away, but eventually.

Doris' philosophy held that she need only record the big ones. Fifteen bucks for gas here twenty for a haircut there—little things like that would surely come out right in the end. I saw her name in the local paper once for third-degree petty theft. Seems she'd rebounded more than a few checks before we got married and her chickens had come home to roost. We had a very long, serious discussion, after which I ended up apologizing.

Doris drove this Pontiac she'd leased right out of college. It was one of those "Hey graduate, have we got a deal for you!" kind of things. Every time she made a late payment, and she made several, they slapped on a fifty-five dollar late fee. I got to know the lady at the finance company on a first-name basis after all the phone calls I fielded on behalf of my spouse.

So, by default, I kept the checkbook for our joint account. My love found my regime a little restrictive, however. Whenever I'd hound her about missing checks and overdrafts, we'd fight like rabid cats and dogs, then subsequently make up like ranch-bred chinchillas.

FREE ADVICE No. 16: New college grads: At about the same time you're avoiding pre-approved credit traps, avoid car salesmen.

As I said, soon after her graduation, some slicker had gotten hold of my beloved and said, "C'mere, sweetie. Have I got a deal for you!" She leased a car. A domestic car. A car with an engine block made of two different metals that do not expand and contract at the same rate when heat is applied to them. A mechanic's nightmare.

With the payments she was making—or not making, as the case may be—over the life of the lease, I figured she would end up paying almost twice what the car was worth and not owning a thing! Is that wild? The idea of a lease is to make it affordable to drive a decent car. What it really does is sucker you into getting more car than you can possibly afford.

I hated that car. I hated the fact that she'd been shanghaied into the deal in the first place. I hated the money it was costing us, and I especially hated the fact that I'd inherited the headache.

Soon after we were married, we got a letter stating that the lease would be up soon and that we had several equally unpalatable options:

(a) We could buy out the lease and pay a premium on a lemon.

(b) We could let it go, leaving us with one vehicle and two, twelve-mile commutes in different directions over iffy farm-to-market roads. Or,

(c) We could hire somebody to drive the thing over a cliff.

I lobbied strongly for option C.

Hey, anybody feel like Chinese?

ABSENTMINDED SWEET/SOUR STIRFRY

Ingredients:

- 2 cups cubed boneless chicken

- 1 can pineapple chunks

- 1 bottle sweet/sour sauce

- Miscellaneous vegetables

- Teriyaki sauce

- Wine vinegar

- Garlic

Directions:

- Marinate chicken in teriyaki, vinegar and garlic; brown in wok on high heat

- Add veggies and stir; cover and steam for about nine mins., making sure to push food up the sides of the wok so it won't burn up.

- Add pineapple chunks, stir two minutes, and serve.

You're asking yourself, "What about the sweet/sour sauce?"

Well, one time I made this for a girlfriend and forgot it. It was still pretty good.

Return of the WASPB

So I asked my wife if she or anyone she knew had a copy of the lease agreement. It seemed logical we find out how much the outrageous balloon payment was going to be. She said she didn't have one.

"No copy of the lease?" I said.

"The man never gave me one," she said.

After a few phone calls, we found out that the balloon would be $4800.00. On top of what she'd already paid, that would have been about $19,000 worth of payments on a $10,000 car! One might be tempted to believe this news put somewhat of a strain on our relationship. One would be correct.

We decided to go with Plan B and turn the thing in, only to find that the car was well over the maximum mileage allowed by the lease, and we could be forced to buy the stupid clunker. We found a sympathetic and slightly unscrupulous dealer who was willing to report the odometer a bit low. Sometimes it pays to live in a small town.

For a time, we operated on one car. In order to get us both to work on time, we had to get up about five in the morning, take the Great Circle Route to the little burg where she taught, drop her off, then I'd proceed across the International Date Line to the tiny, rural high school in which I held court. We then reversed the whole process in the evening. What a hassle! Not to mention the wear and tear on my poor little car, which I'd bought used and paid off more than a year and a half before.

It was about this time I began to doubt some of my recent life decisions. In the car, going home at night, you could have cut the tension with a knife—provided it was a damn sharp one.

We finally agreed to look for a second car. We spent a week planning a foray into the city, checking the ads, and plotting the locations of all the major lots. I'd had some success buying good, used vehicles, and was confident of my ability to find us a serviceable carriage. Imagine my shock and dismay when my darling started climbing into brand-new, twelve and thirteen thousand dollar imports. On teacher's salaries? On *Iowa* teacher's salaries?

Uh-uh. No way. No how.

"But I don't trust used cars," she said.

"Why?" I queried. "Do they have a shifty look about the eyes? Do their palms sweat? What?"

"They always break down."

This from the lady who'd leased the pace car from the Citrus Bowl Parade.

We made several more trips into town, each more dismal than the last. I finally convinced her we couldn't afford anything right from the factory, and that you can get a decent used vehicle with the bugs and the depreciation worked out of them if you try.

Problem was, she didn't know what she wanted and I did. I was looking for a certain Japanese model that my family had had good luck with in the past. Doris knew this, and secretly harbored resentment that I liked the car my mother drove and hated hers.

Then one day, there it was, sitting in the middle of a huge import lot in the pouring rain like a water lily in a swamp. My car.

I begged. I pleaded. She relented. We test-drove it. I checked the mileage, white-gloved the engine, kicked the tires, and pronounced it good. I dickered us a good dicker, too. About a hundred dollars over blue book. We went inside and had the dealer run the financing, although I had every intention of getting the money from my bank at much better interest, and then bringing back a check for the cash amount the next day.

The last straw fell into that poor, overloaded camel's basket right there in the dealer's office. According to the computer, my financial history was satisfactory. However, my dear wife had passed so much bad paper over the years that she couldn't even get credit for having been born. I was furious! Had she ever shared this little tidbit of information with me? Does the Pope wear *lederhosen?*

Something inside of me snapped. I took the following Monday off, and went to my bank to float the loan. When the loan officer, who had handled my college financing and was a friend, said, "Do you want title in both your names or just yours?" I hesitated a split-second. I knew that if I did this, I would be effectively ending my marriage. I took a long deep breath, and let it out slowly.

"My name only," I said.

I was very brave. I left a note in the apartment telling Doris what I'd done and why, and stayed overnight in a motel in town. I sat up eating chips out of a vending machine and playing video games all night.

The next evening, I went home. Doris was out. I started making some goulash for dinner when she came in and slammed the front door. Her lips were drawn so tight I was afraid she'd cut off all circulation to her face. Then she opened her mouth and didn't close it for an hour.

In the process of our "discussion," she threw the remote against the wall, smashing it into a million pieces. I counted them—later. She threw a ladle full of red-hot goulash at me. I ducked, and it splattered all over the kitchen wall, looking like the aftermath of a mob hit in a Sicilian restaurant. Finally, she grabbed me by the facing of the thirty-dollar shirt I was wearing—a gift from my beloved grandmother—and gave it a yank that ripped all the buttons off and sent them flying across the room where they embedded themselves deep in the goulash. I felt this was my cue to leave.

I moved out that evening and never looked back.

FREE ADVICE No. 17: Now pay very close attention. When moving out on a vindictive woman, make sure to take your name off all utilities ASAP Otherwise, get ready for four-figure phone bills to 1-(900) DIAL-A-PSY-CHIC.

DORIS' AIRBORNE GOULASH (In Memoriam)

Ingredients:

- 1 small bag elbow macaroni

- 2 cans condensed tomato soup

- 1 lb. hamburger

- 1 onion, 1 green pepper, 1 clove garlic

Directions:

- Prepare macaroni as per pkg. directions; drain.

- Dump mac and soup into crock-pot.

- Brown burger and drain; add to pot.

- Chop veggies and add to pot.

- Cook on high two hours, on med. five, or on low overnight.

- To test for correct consistency, wing a spoonful across the room and see if it sticks. Serves one.

Free at Last

We tried to work things out, even went to a counselor—separately, of course. But the counselor kept getting off the track and asking about my potty training. A fascinating subject, but hardly relevant. I think they taught her to do that in psych school in order to establish dominance or something. At any rate, the counselor was female, and, at that time, I had about as much confidence in women as Jack the Ripper.

To tell you the truth, Doris was much more willing to work things out than I was. But we each pointed the finger of blame at the other, and guilty or not, a guy can only stand getting the finger for so long.

I was certainly not the ideal husband. There were nights I got so frustrated I would go to my parents' or to a friend's house till late at night, and refuse to account for my whereabouts later on. And, like all great artists, I tended to live a great deal of my life in the realm of fantasy. (Meaning I can be a tremendous liar when it suits me.) Suffice it to say we weren't exactly made for each other.

If Doris wants equal time, she's more than welcome to write her own book.

At nine in the morning, August 20, 1990, I sat in the county court-house waiting to legally sever all ties with my spouse. A high school friend of mine, who is now the local magistrate, came by with his judicial robe open at the front, exposing cutoff shorts and a football jersey underneath, looked at me and said, "What the hell are you doing here?"

"Bill," I said. "Today is the first day of the rest of my life."

An hour later, my father and I set off for the city, three hours away where I'd mercifully landed another teaching job, in a rental truck packed with all my worldly belongings. Some of those belongings I'd never seen before. Since I'd magnanimously left all my old furniture with my ex, my folks had generously purchased a "brand-new," second-hand living room set to help me launch my new life. By three that afternoon we were moving me into my new home-away-from-home.

> FREE ADVICE No. 18—Most good rentals are taken before they ever end up in the newspaper.

I was unaware of this fact until I started checking places out three weeks before I swore out the divorce. I diligently scoured the ads, called up realtors, and tried to crack an incredibly tight rental market.

I'd had plenty of experience renting space in someone's home—none for me this time, thanks—and had my fill of roommates as well. I wanted a place I could call my own. But most situations in my price range were either too far from my new school; attached to somebody's home with lots of kids, elderly relations, or some combination of the two; or were in some way extremely crappy.

Finally, I happened upon three parallel streets near a shopping mall lined with the neatest-looking quad-plexes you ever saw. The location was perfect for getting on the road in the morning, the neighborhood looked nice, and I even ran into an old friend who, it turned out, lived nearby.

I looked for vacancy signs and scanned the paper for corresponding addresses. Bingo! A one-bedroom with appliances, off-street parking, genuine wood paneling, cathedral ceilings. $200 a month! The previous tenant was the landlord's daughter, which lulled me into a false sense of security. After all, what father would let his own kid live in a dump? Well, I hadn't gotten to know my landlord yet.

All seemed well as I moved in. The paneling complemented my furnishings nicely, there was plenty of storage space, and everything mechanical seemed to work. As I settled in, though, I began to notice certain dismaying details. Like the huge water-stain behind the bathroom door, and the soft spot in the floor underneath. Like lines in the ceiling where the panels were nailed directly to the undersides of the roof trusses. And, of course, cockroaches.

The first thunderstorm I experienced was very telling. Wind whistled merrily through the cracks between wall and window casings. A noise like God shuffling a pinochle deck proved to be shingles flapping ten feet above me. And the incoherent screaming above it all turned out not to be ghosts, but my fellow tenants. Seems there was a sheltered workshop for mentally handicapped persons in town. Some of these persons were on an "independent living" program. My neighbors.

I took a closer look at my lease and noticed three letters in fine print at the bottom, which would have told me a great deal had I bothered to read them earlier. The letters were HUD.

Yes, it was a government development, which explained why driving down my street looked like cruising in between two rows of filing cabinets: neat, but unimaginative, and why things seemed to be going wrong one after the other as if on schedule. My landlords were terrific, though. Terrific in the sense that they were always very nice on the phone. Great telephone manners. But I never saw them. I called once to have them come out and fix the toilet.

"Did you jiggle the handle?" Burt said.

"Of course, first thing," I said.

"Did it help?"

"Would I be talking to you if it had?"

"Well, I'll be up sometime next week."

What was I supposed to do in the meantime, cross my legs? I fixed it myself, and billed him for parts.

At one point, the disintegration of the bathroom became too much for even my patient landlords to bear. They asked if I were planning any long trips in the near future so they could get in and replace the tub and shower enclosure. I had caused too much water damage to handle it any other way.

Two weeks after they installed it, the caulk started to peel and the handles on the bathtub spigot began to pull out of the wall. They had ignored the quicksand spot in the floor, which would one day provide me with a handy shortcut downstairs, and apparently decided to let the walls rot out completely to save them the trouble of tearing them out.

They offered to sell me the building once. Actually, they had been trying to unload it for years, and now I knew the reason why. Why did I stay? Well, I guess you could say I found someone even cheaper than my landlords.

I had met the enemy, and he was me.

Actually, despite the fact that there was a lot missing in that place that should have been there, and things that were there that had no business being, I was reasonably happy. Reasonably happy is about what one can expect of my next dish as well:

SHISH-LESS KABOBS

Ingredients:

- 1 pt. fresh mushrooms

- 1 pt. cherry tomatoes

- 1 onion

- 1 green bell pepper

- 1 red bell pepper

- Teriyaki sauce, Worcestershire sauce, rice wine vinegar

Directions:

- Chop onion and peppers into large pieces.

- Marinate all veggies in a mixture of sauces and vinegar for a reasonably long time.

- Impale on wooden skewers, alternating veggies at will. (Better soak the skewers in water first; tell you why in a minute.)

This is great for parties when you're not sure whether or not your guests are carnivorous. I served this to an Indian (from India!) couple once, and they loved it. But if you don't soak the skewers before you put them on the coals, the only one to get skewed will be you.

Tightwad

My primary mission, I decided, was to get myself on my feet financially. I clipped coupons—a habit that is truly profitable.

> FREE ADVICE No. 19: Clipping coupons can easily earn you more per hour than your salary, provided you take paper cuts easily and can put up with the hairy eyeball from your neighbors in the checkout line.

You learn a lot about life clipping coupons. I certainly learned more about the opposite sex than I had even when I was married. Like, I thought yeast was something you used to bake bread or brew beer, not an infection. All these patent medicines on the market to cure it make me suspect some pharmaceutical company genetically engineered a batch of honest, God-fearing yeast into maniacal, disease-ridden vermin just to create a market for their goop.

And every day there are five or six new brands of breakfast cereal. Every time a movie turns out to be a big hit with the kiddies, next day, there's a set of action figures and a breakfast cereal to commemorate it. Instead of an Oscar, the Academy of Motion Picture Arts and Sciences ought to hand out a big bowl of Toasted Oatie-Os to the happy winners.

Anyway, that first fall after the Big Break-Up, I started my new job and was looking for something to do evenings and weekends to make some extra money. I got a part-time job in a hole-in-the-wall music store renting band instruments to prospective young Kenny Gs. I was minding the store one slow Saturday, there was nobody else around, so I started digging through my boss's mammoth collection of business cards. I came up with one that said:

"If I could show you a way to double your income without jeopardizing your present position, would it be worth one hour of your time?"

One hour of *my* time? Certainly. My time was pretty cheap at this particular point in history. I was intrigued. I dialed the 800 number. A jovial answering machine urged me to *take action now!* I left my name and address, as if hypnotized. This was my introduction to the wonderful world of pyramid worship, commonly known as multilevel marketing.

Soon, I was attending these big rah-rah sessions called "opportunity meetings." It was like church, man, it was like being born again. Suddenly, I was very popular with an extremely well-dressed group of people who were all highly motivated, friendly, and accepting. Just what I needed. Never mind that the product was just hair dope and cosmetics. Never mind that I was a straight male with absolutely no experience in sales or cosmetology. Never mind our leader's fantastic resemblance to the Reverend Jim Jones.

I was smart enough never to drink the Kool-Aid.

I suspect there's a lot of money to be made in this sort of thing. Somehow, though, it eluded me. To make it in this business you need the chutzpah of a repo man and the morals of a whore. Oh, I did pretty well in retail sales. I got my whole family hooked on all these totally unique, revolutionary products like shampoo, soap, and lipstick. I did have a few customers who were no relation to me, and if I'd left it at that, I might have made a few bucks.

But one of the higher-ups in my group was a big-time cosmetic surgeon—very charismatic—and had his eye on me as "executive material." Between him and my sponsor, they had me eating up all my free time and available credit balance recruiting new "independent distributors." I was going broke buying starter kits while the volume on their computer sheets loomed larger and larger.

At one point, I had a group volume of over three thousand dollars worth of product sold in one month—just me and those I had signed up working in our spare time. My bonus check for all that was about eighty bucks. And my expenses were way closer to my group volume than to my commission. But somehow, I was convinced that the Big Money was just around the corner.

One night, my "upline" executive called me. "Jeff, buddy..." he said. I hate being called "buddy," but from him it sounded like I was being knighted.

"Jeff, buddy, have I got news for you! We're all going on a cruise!"

"We are?" I said breathlessly.

"You bet! 'The Company' is booking half a cruise ship—one of the big 'Love Boats'—for a four-day training cruise to the Bahamas. You ever been to the Bahamas, buddy?"

I told him I hadn't.

"Well, you're going now. It's only eight hundred bucks, and it's all tax-deductible!"

Now, the last steady job this man had had was as a floor salesman. Literally, he sold floors in a carpet store for his ex-brother-in-law. What did he know from tax-deductible?

So, I went on a Caribbean cruise in the middle of August. It was great! We spent the night before our flight to Miami in a hot tub in Des Moines with everybody in our group. The spa was parked in back of a beautiful three-story home belonging to a retired insurance exec and his wife who were into the business, but smart enough to keep it on a cash basis.

We had a celebration dinner at a fancy restaurant and drinks in several places before hitting the tub, with me flashing plastic everywhere and pocketing the receipts for my taxes. The next morning, we were off.

The cruise was fantastic. We swam, we snorkeled, we ogled babes in bikinis and less. We drank like fish and ate like hogs. In between gluttony sessions, we attended these very serious "seminars" that would have sparked nostalgia in the heart of an old Maoist. The doctrine and attitude adjustment were thick and glittery, with big executive distributors testifying to their success stories, giving each other achievement awards while we cheered and praised them as if they were pagan idols.

I got to talk to a few of them offstage, though. It seemed like the ones raking in the big money all had it to start with, and most of them had made it in legitimate business. When I asked one of them why he had quit to do this he said, "Because I got tired of working so hard." That got me to thinking: "Who was doing all his work for him now?"

Me, that's who. Me and all the other greedy slobs who were getting fleeced because we let our adrenal glands do our thinking for us. I decided to enjoy the rest of my cruise, go home, and close up shop.

So I went to a tax office a few months later, having carefully matched each receipt with a cancelled check or credit slip, armed with a finicky spreadsheet detailing each and every expenditure that had any connection at all with my side-business. My income for the year: $917.34. My expenses: close to $5000! How much of it was actually deductible? About a thousand. None of it from the cruise.

"This 'training cruise'," the skinny little part-time tax preparer said, peering over his pince-nez. "Was it mandatory?"

"Well…no."

"Could you have gotten the same 'training' elsewhere, without incurring these incidental expenses?"

"Well…yes."

"Was the entire cruise conducted within U.S. waters?"
"Well...no."
"Was the ship of U.S. registry?"
"How should I know?"
"I'm sorry, not allowable."

Not allowable. Ditto the computer I'd bought; ditto the boombox I'd purchased in order to listen to subliminal motivational tapes; ditto the voice mail. Why didn't somebody tell me before I'd buried myself in plastic?

FREE ADVICE No. 20: If it sounds too good to be true, it's petty larceny at the very least.

Epilogue: A couple of days ago, I heard from my "upline" guy for the first time in over a year. He called me up saying he just wanted to "catch up with what I was doing."

"You still doing that writing, buddy?" he said.
"Yes. I'm working on my second book."
"Hey, that's terrific. Say, I just wanted to let you know—we've stumbled onto something a hundred times better than 'The Company.' Some folks are gonna make a lot of money if they get in early..."

One thing I did learn from "The Company" is the power of hype. That's the rationale behind the title of my next recipe. Well, part of the rationale anyway. The rest has to do with its aftereffects:

JEFF'S JUMPIN' JACK FLASH JAZZ BEANS

Ingredients:

- Two lg. cans pork & beans

- One lg. red onion

- One sm. bottle mesquite-flavored barbecue sauce

- ½ cup honey

- Two tbsps. brown sugar

- ½ clove garlic

- Cajun spice, chili powder or ground cayenne pepper

Directions:

- Open beans and place in lg. saucepan.

- Mince entire onion and stir in.

- Add BBQ sauce, honey, sugar, and spice.

- Cook on med. high until bubbly.

Very robust! I would recommend, however, that you seat guests a respectful distance apart from one another, and keep everyone away from open flame.

Manual Labor

So I returned every bit of excess product I had to "The Company" (for 90 percent of cost). That refund, my tax refund, and everything else I could scrape together for the next several months went to pay off my credit cards. So much for free enterprise.

I started to look for ways to save a few shekels. I noticed that, along with everything else that was coming apart in my building and its twin across the parking lot, both barns needed a serious coat of paint. I'd done a lot of house painting over the years, my dad owned a paint sprayer, and there were so few windows on these structures that I thought I could make them shipshape and Bristol fashion in no time. I called my landlord, who was apparently thinking along the same lines and undoubtedly looking for a cheap way out.

We agreed on eight months free rent if I would paint both buildings. He opened an account for me at the paint store, I got my supplies—my sprayer, my paint—and went to work the beginning of June. I could see loose, peeling paint under the eaves, so I climbed to the top of the 28-foot extension ladder I'd bought (on credit) at Sears because the one Burt lent me was somewhat less than stable. I scraped my way across the top of both buildings. It took me two weeks—half the time spent dodging wasps and angry, displaced pigeons.

I was also temporarily stymied when I discovered both buildings were 30 feet high at their peak—difficult to manage with a 28-foot ladder. I ended up duct-taping my scraper to the end of a broom handle. This apparatus came in quite handy the day a big gust of wind came up out of nowhere, and I was forced to use it for balance like Karl Wallenda working without a net. I had to go in and change my shorts when I finally got down safely.

There were only tiny spots of loose paint on the walls themselves. It looked like an easy job. But when I scraped my first dot, my scraper slipped and I heard a soft "pop" as the corner punctured the paper covering of the exterior wallboard, known in the building trade as "buffalo board." The wall was nothing but paper and brown fiber! Some shelter. Not only that, but the loose dots of paint turned out to be the flat heads of building nails—building nails that were about a foot apart all over the walls. I made a rough count and came up with a figure of about 1800 nail heads per wall, with an itty-bitty dot of peeling paint on each. I gritted my teeth for a solid month of tedious scraping.

So now both apartment buildings sported a fascinating pattern of shiny specks where the sun glinted off bare nail heads. I filled my sprayer with primer and primed the underside of the eaves in two days. No sweat.

For the dots, however, I used a roller attached to my trusty broom handle. I found I could stand halfway up the ladder and do a neat block of dots a double arm's-length on either side. But it was slow work, and the pattern of dots made me dizzy. When I had an entire front wall done, I went a little loony and began to connect the dots with white primer. I did a flower, a clown and a spaceship. I did a nifty self-portrait in three-quarter profile. Then I began to *realize* I'd gone crazy, and painted "HELP ME" in big block letters across the front of my building. My landlord was not pleased.

Finally, I was ready to spray some paint. I cut some cardboard and taped plastic sheeting to it to cover the windows. It didn't occur to me until I was twenty feet above ground just how good a sail a sheet of cardboard covered with plastic sheeting can be. Fortunately, I let go of it before the top of the ladder leaned too far away from the side of the building.

> FREE ADVICE No. 21: A healthy respect for the weather is a key attribute of the successful housepainter.

I had this idea in mind that the velocity with which my sprayer propelled paint plus the viscosity of the paint itself would serve to negate any lateral force of wind. This idea proved incorrect.

The windows were covered. I had nothing but clear wall space and a cool sunny day ahead of me. My boombox sat under a tree with a stack of "talking books" next to it. I figured I'd catch up on my trashy horror novels while I worked. Sure there was a slight breeze, but so what?

The first spray flew back in my face and painted my glasses a lovely redwood hue. No, I wasn't wearing protective goggles, either.

I climbed down twenty feet completely blind, with a four-pound paint sprayer in one hand, a full can of paint in the other, and two hundred feet of power cord over my shoulder. The wind came up and made my aluminum ladder hum like a harp-string beneath my feet. After what seemed like the pregnant pause before Judgment Day, I made it to Earth, cleaned my glasses, drank a beer and took the rest of the day off.

I changed my system somewhat after that—invested in some protective eyewear, gauged the wind before ascending—that sort of thing. I made much better progress, subsequently.

As I crawled around the buildings like Spider-Man on his day off, I noticed certain things about them that disturbed me. There were small,

cantilevered metal terraces that were meant to serve as fire escapes—I
guess you were just supposed to jump the ten feet to the ground since
there were no stairs. The outer corners of each were supported by two
long four-by-fours set in concrete footings in the ground. But the very
large bolts connecting these uprights to the underside of the terraces
were all completely rusted away. I broke into a cold sweat thinking
about all the barbequing and sunbathing I'd done up there.

I resolved to avoid the terraces until they were repaired, which is to
say, I'm still avoiding them. I figured if I ever needed to get down to
the first floor in a hurry, I could just jump up and down in the bathroom till the soft spot in the floor gave way.

Of course, the first thing my parents do when they visit is look for
danger. My mother somehow intuited my discovery of that deathtrap
of a terrace. On a weekend visit, she made a beeline for it, completely
unprompted. She rhapsodized loud and long about how I must be care-
ful and point these things out to my landlord, that HUD should be
contacted, and so on, all the while jumping up and down on the terrace
to confirm that, yes, it was inches from plummeting to the ground.
Apparently, she thought she herself was immune to gravity. I suppose
most moms do.

The next recipe goes without saying.

MOTHER'S PICKLED TONGUE

Ingredients:

- 1 beef tongue

- Vinegar

- Pickling spice

Directions:

- Place beef tongue in boiling water till it turns all pasty white.

- Peel off skin.

- Pickle in vinegar and pickling spice using standard pickling techniques available from other cookbooks or from the nearest little old lady. (Do I have to lay everything out for you?)

- Slice for sandwiches.

This one clearly speaks for itself.

Here and Now

Sure, I've had a lot of fun living where I live. Like when I came home from my first day of teaching, as I pulled into my parking spot, I saw a furry orange streak zip across the yard, and under the front steps.

I got out and peered under the stairs. Nothing. I poked a stick between the concrete stoop and the foundation and heard a faint squeak. I made a point to try to spot the critter as I pulled in each day, but like Bigfoot, whatever it was remained elusive and just beyond reach. I finally caught my first clear glimpse of it by parking on the street and tiptoeing across the lawn. There was a fat, orange guinea pig living under the front steps of my building.

I inquired of my independently living neighbors, who told me that one of their friends had had to move out earlier in the spring and couldn't take her pet with her. So she set it free. Her caseworker called the animal shelter, but the little fuzzball had successfully dodged their live-traps all summer. I anthropomorphically began to refer to the little guy as "Bucky."

His legend grew over the weeks that followed. The folks in my carpool adopted him as sort of a mascot. Then the Animal Rescue League came out in full force. I guess they must have contacted my erstwhile landlords and gotten permission to put these hideous, spring-loaded boxes all around the foundation. They looked like the showers at Auschwitz.

But the Buckster was too smart for 'em. Once I actually saw him tiptoe in after the pile of grain they used for bait, turn around and emerge unscathed, the trap unsprung. I swear he gave that thing the guinea-pig finger before darting back into his shelter with his fuzzy amber cheeks stuffed with high-grade field corn.

I didn't see or hear from him for two whole weeks after that. Suddenly, the traps were gone. I went into a period of mourning that simmered slowly into anger.

"How dare they?" I thought. By what right did they take away an innocent rodent's freedom just because he was supposed to be domestic? They claimed it was for the animal's own good, but Bucky had been doing just fine under the steps, thank you very much, and if he had died there, at least he would have died free.

I drew a pretty good picture of him with the caption "FREE BUCKY" in bold calligraphy, and posted photocopies all over both buildings. One day, there he was again, sitting up on the stoop, small as life, nibbling grass with a sly grin on his face as if to say "Just laying low till the heat was off, Bud."

I nearly wept for joy.

One evening a week or so later, however, I was out grilling hamburgers when I heard this horrible chirp and squeal of pain coming from deep inside a forsythia bush. I didn't want to look, being sober enough to realize it was not the bush itself.

Sure enough, I haven't seen Bucky since. But at least I have the memories, and the certainty that Bucky died as he lived, proud, free, and brave.

Other fun things happen at my place as well. Like every time a storm knocks the power out during the night, my neighbors panic, and I make the rounds like Santa Claus lending them all flashlights and candles, and try to get them to quit screaming.

Oh, and then there was the time I called my ex and asked her out for nostalgia's sake. Oh my, yes, I had a good laugh that time.

Sadly, we have come to our final recipe. As with all endings, partings of ways and bon voyages, we have a choice either to be sad, or to celebrate. I personally choose to celebrate because this book has been a lot more work than I'd originally thought. It's been all I could do just to come up with clever chapter titles, let alone eighteen different and wholeheartedly delectable recipes. Try it sometime, you'll see.

JEFF'S JOYFUL JUNGLE JUICE

Ingredients:

- 1 lg. plastic kitchen wastebasket, previously unused

- 1 gal. unsweetened orange juice

- 2 qts. club soda

- 1 fifth lime vodka

- 1 fifth lemon schnapps

- 1 fifth grapefruit liqueur

Directions:

Wash out wastebasket thoroughly.
Mix all ingredients, stirring briskly.

Serves an entire fraternity, two golf foursomes, the starting lineup of the average slow-pitch softball team and their dates. I learned this one in college, and we're back where we started.

Chapter Twenty

I've got no complaints these days. True, I live in the same hovel I've been beefing about for the last three chapters, but it's been taken over recently by people who know how to use tools. Of course, the rent has gone up, but if they're actually going to put a floor under my floor, it'll be worth it.

Amazing, I've come to the end of this book and didn't even realize it. I'd intended to get off these rambling reminiscences and do a chapter or two on how to use foliage plants to make your apartment look like less of a poverty pocket, or on some of my favorite household substances. Baking soda, for example.

Wonderful stuff, baking soda. You can bathe in it, brush your teeth with it, wash clothes in it, stick it in your fridge to alleviate that dead-fish-and-onions aroma, sprinkle it on your shag before vacuuming, put it under a cat or a bird, cook with it, cure a hangover with it, or mix it with vinegar for a nifty science project. It's cheap, too. You can fill a grocery cart with it and still have lottery money left. And it's the one thing on Earth you can feel absolutely secure about buying an off-brand.

There's no designer baking soda—no taste tests where five out of ten proctologists recommend baking soda for their patients' piles. No bikini bimbos trying to make you feel inadequate as a man for not using their sponsor's product. There are no illegal baking soda pushers on the streets, no international terrorist cabals raising money for gray-market armaments by smuggling baking soda across state lines, no soulless, materialistic yuppies snorting baking soda through rolled-up hundred-dollar bills.

All in all, a most admirable product.

But it looks like I won't have time for that. I would like to say, though, that I'm sorry this didn't turn out to be quite the "Handy Household Hints" book you might have expected. Or some kind of touchy-feely, self-help guru sort of thing. I intended to write such a book—I really did. But all this stuff kept cropping up and, well, I sort of got sidetracked.

Or maybe I didn't. Maybe you can take these restless, dissatisfied maunderings as sort of an example—a bad example, certainly—of how one guy stumbled blindly through his young adult years and lived to tell about it. Too bad hardly anybody ever learns by example, but by stupid, painful experience. If they did, then maybe you could avoid the mistakes I've made, some of which were a lot of fun, but many not.

But if you insist, I'll break it down for you:

Stay close to your family. They're the ones who'll always be there, even when they'd rather be in Orlando.

Stay close to your friends. They may come in handy when you need a place to hide out from your family.

Be honest and open in your relationships. Tell her what you need and want. If she loves you, she'll listen. If you love her, so will you.

Trust your heart, but use your head.

Pay cash or do without.

Don't yell so much.

That's about it.

Oh, the recipes. Like I said, most of them are edible if you're not too fussy. Remember, God and your grandmother hate a picky eater. The best thing to do, though, is find someone to do at least half the cooking, and marry her.

You heard me. Yes, I'm looking in that general direction again. Funny, isn't it? After all, "Once bitten, twice shy." But somehow, having screwed it up royally once has made me even more anxious to do it right the next time. I'm seeing a wonderful woman right now, maybe...

I'll let you know when the *WASP Guide to a Happy Marriage* comes out.

0-595-32447-9

22838528R00074

Made in the USA
Middletown, DE
09 August 2015